Leadership Plain and Simple

Leadership
Plain and
Simple
Second edition

Steve Radcliffe

Edited by Anthony Landale

PEARSON

Harlow, England • London • New York • Boston • San Francisco • Toronto • Sydney
Auckland • Singapore • Hong Kong • Tokyo • Seoul • Taipei • New Delhi
Cape Town • São Paulo • Mexico City • Madrid • Amsterdam • Munich • Paris • Milan

PEARSON EDUCATION LIMITED

Edinburgh Gate
Harlow CM20 2JE
Tel: +44 (0)1279 623623
Fax: +44 (0)1279 431059
Website: www.pearson.com/uk

First published in Great Britain in 2010
Second edition 2012

Pearson Education is not responsible for the content of third-party internet sites.

ISBN: 978-0-273-77241-5

British Library Cataloguing-in-Publication Data
A catalogue record for this book is available from the British Library

Library of Congress Cataloging-in-Publication Data
Radcliffe, Steve.
  Leadership plain and simple / Steve Radcliffe ; edited by Anthony Landale. -- 2nd ed.
      p. cm.
  Includes bibliographical references and index.
  ISBN 978-0-273-77241-5 (pbk.)
1. Leadership. I. Landale, Anthony. II. Title.
  HD57.7.R333 2012
  658.4'092--dc23

                    20122006724

10 9 8 7 6 5 4 3 2 1
15 14 13 12

Typeset in 9pt Helvetica Neue 57 Condensed by 3
Printed and bound in Great Britain by Henry Ling Ltd, Dorchester, Dorset

Contents

Foreword

These are cynical times. It is easy to begin to believe that there is nothing new under the sun and that innovative ideas are actually inconsequential updates on ancient managerial wisdom.

We don't believe that. Indeed, we have been fortunate over the past 25 years to have worked with some of the world's greatest business thinkers – from Peter Drucker to Kjell Nordstrom and Jonas Ridderstrale by way of Warren Bennis and Charles Handy. We now compile a ranking of business gurus – the Thinkers 50 (**www.thinkers50.com**) – which seeks to identify the business thinker who is making the most significant contribution to how managers in the field actually run their businesses.

And this is why cynicism is misplaced: business ideas actually change the way businesses are managed. As we speak, someone is devouring the latest book from CK Prahalad, Malcolm Gladwell, or indeed one of our own books, and thinking how they can put the ideas to work in their own organisation.

Business books are unique and uniquely demanding. Readers expect a pay-off. They anticipate an actionable idea, something they can bring to next Tuesday's marketing meeting.

That's why Steve Radcliffe is worth reading and worth listening to.

We were disappointingly late converts to Steve's world. He crept under our radar. Indeed, Steve has been operating outside the reach of managerial radar for many years. Quietly and unobtrusively, Steve and his team have been making a profound difference to the lives of leaders in an array of organisations – from Niall Fitzgerald at Unilever to Sir Gus O'Donnell in the Cabinet Office and hundreds of others. Until now, Steve has been leadership's best kept secret.

No more. With typical off-the-radar, let's-get-on-with-it enthusiasm, Steve published his own book in 2008. It captured his *Future–Engage–Deliver* model which, as with any great model, is easily understood and incredibly demanding. As Steve's house became a book warehouse and a procession of boxes were dispatched, the phone started ringing even more insistently and hasn't stopped since. E-mails arrived from headteachers and medical officers who'd tried out the ideas. Business leaders, too, got in touch because Steve's approach resonated with their reality.

People loved the book. And that's the thing about Steve's approach: it is accessible to people in the real world of work and is intent on making a difference to their lives. The book became a buzz and now a real movement for change in the way we think about and practise leadership.

There is a freshness and enthusiasm to Steve Radcliffe's work that dispels cynicism. Working with Steve, we have found that what we stand for, how and why we work, and where we want to be, has come into much sharper focus. In the end it is down to each of us to make a difference in our own lives and those of others we live and work with. Steve Radcliffe can help you make a difference.

Stuart Crainer & Des Dearlove
Visiting Professors, IE Business School, creators of the Thinkers 50 and
bestselling authors

Introduction to the Second Edition

Welcome to the second edition of *Leadership: Plain and Simple*. When I first wrote and self-published the book a few years ago, I thought that at least it would be a good record of my thinking about leadership. As it is, here is the second edition published by Financial Times Publishing and it's turned out to be a hit!

It's been the number one book of the 50,000+ offered in the search for 'leadership' on Amazon UK for over a year now. And readers have added over 100 five-star reviews, more than for any other business book on the site, ever.

The book seems to have a struck a chord in a couple of ways. First, it's not a book about theory. It's about an approach we call Future–Engage–Deliver or FED that you can instantly make real for yourself and use practically. Second, it debunks all that stuff about leadership being complicated and only for a chosen few. It invites us all into seeing ourselves as leaders and encourages us to see we can all be more confident, calm, effective or whatever we choose.

The Times describes FED as the 'no-nonsense approach ... shaking up the world of leadership'. One of the ways we want to shake up the thinking about leadership is to have more people see that what organisations need in difficult times is leadership at all levels, not just at the top. This may not have been a priority when times were good, budgets were increasing and growth was easy to come by. But times are tougher now and for most organisations it simply isn't good enough to have a few 'leaders' at the top transmitting messages to the rest of us.

What's most pleasing for us is that we're making progress encouraging this new thinking in the worlds of health, education, the arts and charities as well as business and the civil service. I'm delighted that we are helping teachers, doctors, nurses, civil servants and others see how they can step forward as leaders, regardless of their job title or position.

To help stimulate this thinking even more, in this second edition, I've added a new chapter on how FED can be used to make a difference throughout all your organisation. I hope also you'll gain strength from some new, inspiring stories of people stepping forward as leaders in a whole range of situations.

As we say on the cover, 'Anyone can be a leader. Here's how.'

Steve Radcliffe, February 2012

A Very Big 'Thank You'

I've been lucky to have a fabulous Support Team. There are so many people I want to thank for their contribution to my growth and development. First, many thanks to those who have hired us and given us the chance to learn our trade. This includes:

Sarah Alexander	Chief Executive and Artistic Director, National Youth Orchestra
Andy Anson	CEO, England 2018, The Football Association
Richard Baker	Chief Executive, Alliance Boots, and now Chairman, Virgin Active and DFS
Fergus Balfour	CEO, Unilever Cosmetics International
Vindi Banga	President, Unilever Foods
John Barbour	CEO, ToysRUs.com
Jeremy Bevan	Head of EMEAR Marketing, Cisco International
Richard Bevan	Chief Executive, League Managers Association
Kay Bews	Chief Executive, Homestart
Andy Bird	Managing Director, Brand Learning
Ian Bradley	Chief Executive, Mattel Canada
Hugh Burkitt	Chief Executive, The Marketing Society
Kate Carty	Chief Crown Prosecutor, Nottinghamshire
Natalie Ceeney	Chief Executive, The National Archives and now Financial Ombudsman Service
Sir Suma Chakrabarti	Permanent Secretary, Ministry of Justice
Rita Clifton	Chair, Interbrand UK
John Coombs	Managing Director, Unilever Ventures
Geoffrey Dennis	Chief Executive, CARE International
Robert Devereux	Permanent Secretary, Department of Work and Pensions

Andy Duncan	Marketing Director, BBC and Chief Executive, Camelot
Iain Ferguson	Chief Executive, Birds Eye Walls and Tate & Lyle
Ian Filby	Director, Alliance Boots and Chief Executive, DFS
Niall Fitzgerald	Chairman, Unilever and Reuters
Mark Fladrich	VP Global Brands, Astra Zeneca
Rob Forshaw	Managing Partner, Grand Union
Simon Freedman	Head of Marketing, Football Association and Lucozade
Adam Freeman	Executive Director, Commercial, Guardian News & Media
John Garfield	Chief Executive, John Charcol
David Garman	Chief Executive, Allied Bakeries and TDG plc
Paddy Gaul	Managing Partner, Weightmans
Dr Paul Golby	Chief Executive, Eon UK
Richard Greenhalgh	Chairman, CARE International and First Milk
Dominic Grounsell	Marketing Director, Capitol One and More Than
John Harper	President, Hasbro Europe
Kevin Havelock	President, Refreshment Category, Unilever
John Heaps	Chairman, Eversheds
Professor David Hopkins	Professor of Education, Nottingham University
Denis Horton	Chief Executive, Fisher-Price
Neil Hufton	Chief Executive, Diversey Lever
Peter Humphreys	Chief Executive, First Milk
Monica Jacobs	Chair, Homestart Havant
Peter Knight	Chairman, CEO Circle
Peter Lees	Founding Director, Faculty of Medical Leadership and Management of the UK Medical Royal Colleges
Rob Lucas	Chief Executive, Turley Associates
John McAdam	Chief Executive, Unichema and ICI
Andrew McDonald	Chief Executive, Government Skills

Dame Mavis McDonald	Permanent Secretary, Office of the Deputy Prime Minister
Amanda Mackenzie	Chief Marketing Officer, Aviva and President, The Marketing Society
Mhairi McEwan	Managing Director, Brand Learning
Alistair McGeorge	Chief Executive, Littlewoods and Matalan
Roger Maslin	Managing Director, Wembley Stadium
Gavin Neath	Chairman, Van den Bergh Foods
Matt Nicholls	Managing Partner, Grand Union
Una O'Brien	Permanent Secretary, Department of Health
Sir Gus O'Donnell	Cabinet Secretary and Head of the Civil Service
Jim O'Sullivan	Managing Director, Edinburgh Airport
Chris Pilling	Chief Executive, First Direct and Yorkshire Building Society
Sir Michael Pitt	Chief Executive, Kent County Council
Heather du Quesnay	Chief Executive, National College for School Leadership
Alan Raymant	Chief Operating Officer, Horizon Nuclear Power
Alan Reade	Executive Chairman, Merial Pharmaceuticals
Dame Fiona Reynolds	Director General, The National Trust
Christopher Selsby	Managing Director, Harwood International, Europe
Minouche Shafik	Permanent Secretary, Department for International Development
Sir Kevin Smith	Chief Executive, GKN
Nigel Stein	Chief Executive, GKN
Paul Thurston	Chief Executive, Retail Banking and Wealth Management, HSBC
Lord Turnbull	Cabinet Secretary and Head of the Civil Service
Neil Ward	Acting Chief Executive, HM Courts Service
Keith Weed	Chief Marketing and Communication Officer, Unilever
Scott Wheway	Retail Director, Alliance Boots

plus many others in these organisations as well as UK Government Ministers and people at the National School of Government, The Cabinet Office, the Crown Prosecution Service, Henley College, Cambridge University and on the UK Government Think Tank on the Development of Leadership in Schools.

Many thanks, too, to those in these organisations who've made a special contribution to my development. At the top of my list are John Byrne, Didier Dallemagne, Hilary Douglas, Stephen Lehane, David Macleod, Tony Pearce, Chris Pote, Tony Smith, Giorgina Soane and Tim Stacey.

I absolutely couldn't have written this book without the learning and partnership I've had from my colleagues over the years. A special thank you goes to Vic Crew, Alison and Bill McCabe, and Dominic, Maggie and Tony Turnbull of The McLane Group. Hale Dwoskin, Mike Eales and Charlie Smith, thanks for your wisdom. And Steve Core, Werner Holzmann, Alan Humphries, Lucy Kidd, Anthony Landale, Ian Lock, John Pringle and Anni Townend, thanks for your partnership.

Then there are the friends who've been a great support to me along the way. A big thanks to Alyssa Abbey, Jim Boxall, Simon and Gaye Callaghan, Sue Cosens, John and Gill Harper, Janet and Steve Hughes, Art Kaplan, Ronald and Jean Redhead, Tony Reiss, Bim and Katie Verrechia and Peter Waller.

I've had great help creating the early self-published edition of this book. Thanks to editor, Anthony Landale, and designer, Steve Hobbs, and to Jim Boxall, Alister Scott and Anni Townend. Many thanks to Liz Gooster and Eloise Cook from Pearson for helping produce this version. And to Des Dearlove and Stuart Crainer, thanks for your wise counsel. Thanks also to those whose stories appear in the case studies in this edition.

And the biggest thanks of all go to my brilliant gang at home: Sharron, Nic, Alex and Sophie. Thanks for your love and patience with Daddio!

Publisher's acknowledgement

The distinctions in the Relationship to Results Pyramid were derived from Landmark Education copyrighted materials and are used with permission. All rights reserved.

Welcome

... this 'leadership stuff' really needn't be complicated.

Welcome

One of my great passions is helping people grow as leaders. Why? Because I've seen so often the difference that quality leadership can make to the lives of people and the success of organisations.

I've written this book with the sole purpose of helping you develop faster as a more confident, capable leader. The only qualification you need is the desire to grow.

But let me be clear right up front. When I say 'leadership', I don't mean the leadership that comes from position or title. What I mean by leadership is you being at your best, in touch with what you care about and doing something about it. Where I'm coming from after 20 years in this field is simple and clear: everyone can be a leader and make a bigger difference whether it's to your career, your performance, the relationships you have with colleagues or the quality of life you have at home.

It absolutely doesn't matter where you are in an organisation. You can be in your first job, you can have no direct reports. You can have a team or run a department. You can head an organisation. And you can work in a school, hospital, charity or global business. It really doesn't matter because I've seen inspiring leadership from people in all these positions and I've realised that the fundamentals of leadership are the same for any situation.

We'll explore these fundamentals together in this book and I'll share with you the ideas and practices I've seen that have most helped people grow as leaders. You'll learn more about the leader you are now, the leader you want to be and the ways of getting there, even if you don't yet fully think of yourself as a leader.

What I'll bring will come from my journey as both a leader and partner to other leaders. After my early years in Wigan in the north of England, at Oxford University and then Procter & Gamble, I moved to the USA to be a chief executive in a multinational business before returning to the UK.

I then realised that who I wanted to be was a great partner to leaders. So for 20 years now, I've been a leadership coach and consultant to individuals, teams and organisations of all shapes and sizes.

I've learned lots from reading other books on leadership but my most enlightening learning has come from sitting alongside leaders in 'live' situations as they have worked at engaging and mobilising others. I have captured what I've learned in my proven approach to developing leaders, *Future–Engage–Deliver*, the only three leadership practices you'll ever need.

I've seen that there is real value in keeping messages straightforward and practical. And this is what I'll do in this book.

This 'leadership stuff' really needn't be complicated. I believe that leading is a natural, human activity that is a part of all of us. You don't need a certain IQ or job title to be a leader!

But there is something you do need. You need to be 'up to something'. That is, you need to have an ambition, dream or goal for your team, organisation, colleagues or yourself and it's got to matter to you.

I've been a partner to hundreds of leaders and this has been the only common feature among them – whether we've been focusing on private or public sector challenges, in crisis or quieter times, on a local or global scale – the leader has wanted a different future and was determined to do something about it. He or she was 'up to something' that mattered to them.

This is so important. Do not have all your focus on your competencies and skills. First and foremost, get in touch with what you care about and want to be 'up to'. Then make it happen.

At this moment, you may not be clear on what you're 'up to'. That's perfectly ok. I'll help you get clearer on this.

Or you may be pretty clear on what's important to you and what you want but you don't know how you're going to make it happen. That's ok, too, and has been the case at some time with everyone I've worked with.

Or you may not even allow yourself to think about the future because you are not confident you can influence it. Well, I'll encourage you to throw yourself in, try new approaches, experiment, practise and learn. In particular, I'll urge you to be really open to learning about yourself, and understand what it is about you that brings people with you and makes things happen. And also how you at times hold yourself back and so limit what's possible.

The result of you taking this approach is that you are guaranteed to become an even more confident and effective leader. I will show you ways you can immediately handle some situations differently and be more the leader you want to be. However, you will not grow fully as a leader overnight. It's something that takes time and comes with practice. My ambition is to be your partner in this endeavour. So please do not think of this as just a stand-alone book to be read once. There will be value in you returning to it often. Here's how I suggest you best use the book:

First, read at least the next chapter to get an overview of the topic of leadership.

> *I believe one of the factors holding many of us back from growing as leaders is that we don't have an overall grasp of what it's all about. Many of us have a number of ideas about leadership without seeing how they all fit together.*

Second, when you're ready, read the book to identify what sort of leader you want to be and how you currently are as a leader. You will be naturally strong and not so strong in some aspects of leadership – that's how we all are. Get a sense of this as you read and begin clarifying how you want to grow.

Third, dip in at any time when things are not going well. Use this book to help you identify what's going on and what aspect of leadership is missing – I promise you the answer's in here!

Also use the book when things are going well. That way you can learn about what's really making things work and you can then take this learning to other situations.

The book is just one part of support for your ongoing development. For instance, at the website **www.futureengagedeliver.com** you can subscribe to regular, free postings of articles, podcasts and videos that will keep you up to date with *Future–Engage–Deliver*. At **www.futureengagedeliver.com/book** you'll see copies of the key pages of the book which you can print off to carry as prompts or share with colleagues. You'll also find quotes and articles that have inspired me and that may inspire you too.

And please don't keep this stuff to yourself. Part of what you care about may be helping others to grow as leaders. In which case, get them involved. Talk to them about what you're learning. Help them get in touch with what they care about and how they'd like to grow as leaders. Steer them to the webpage. Give them a copy of the book!

Finally, let me hear back from you. If you have comments or stories to share, please send them to me. And if you want more support, there is a team of us who can support you by phone or by coming to see you.

I've distilled my learnings about leadership into a simple yet powerful framework, *Future–Engage–Deliver*. It captures the very best ideas and the three practices of how to grow faster as a leader. *Leadership: Plain and Simple* brings the framework to life so you can make it real for you and rapidly accelerate your development as a leader who makes a difference.

Future–Engage–Deliver

... there are only three aspects to leading that you've got to grasp. They are Future, Engage, Deliver.

- Future–Engage–Deliver
  - First, leading always starts in the Future
  - Second, if you want the help of others to create that Future, you'll need to Engage them
  - And third, in Deliver, you make things happen
- What do you see about your Organisation?
- What do you see about You?

Future–Engage–Deliver

In this chapter, you'll see that all this 'leadership stuff' needn't be as complicated as it's often made out to be.

And you'll see that you already have what you need to be an effective leader.

Boy, have I been slow?! For years, I've read all the latest books on people, leadership and organisations. Why? Because I've been seduced into thinking that this leadership stuff is really complicated, even mysterious. And I believed I'd have to do lots of reading to really 'get it'.

A major error! In contrast, when I've reflected on what it was about the leadership that switched on that board, project team or warehouse operator, I've recognised that there have always been three ingredients at play:

Future–Engage–Deliver

This is the model I have proven in use with leaders the world over. It has consistently been the catalyst for leaders who have wanted to accelerate their own and others' growth. It really is that simple – I promise you that you'll find a place for any leadership idea you come across inside this framework.

The fact is that whether you want to organise a great birthday party, create a high-performing team or help build a society that prospers, all you'll need to practise are these three aspects of leading.

Of course, it may not be easy to be brilliant at all three aspects, but I promise you that these ideas are all you need to 'get' in order to grow your leadership. Let me explain.

> "It was only later that I came to see that you have to oversimplify things sometimes in order to begin to understand them. Only when the basic frameworks are established can you add in the qualifications and complexities."
>
> Charles Handy

First, leading always starts in the Future

Leading always starts with ideas and thoughts about what you'd like to see in the Future, how you'd like things to be, where you'd like to get to or what you'd like to build.

We have many words to describe these ideas; they include 'goal, target, ambition, aspiration, dream' and from the world of business you can add words like 'vision, mission, direction and strategic intent'. These are all ways of describing the Future you want.

I'll say a lot more about Future later but let me be absolutely clear right now:

Powerful and effective leaders are guided by the Future they want. And more than this, the leader is strongest when that Future is powerfully connected to what he or she cares about.

Why does this matter? Because the more commitment the leader has for the desired future, the more they will persist, the more energy they'll bring along the way, the more they'll stay 'up to something'.

Additionally, when the leader has this powerful relationship to the Future they care about, it can also have an extraordinary impact on others … sparking innovative thinking, giving people a reason to go the extra mile, providing hope in times of difficulty and, most importantly, giving meaning to people's work. In essence, a strong connection to the Future you want can create a mood of optimism, hope and possibility that can ignite human creativity and build confidence.

Second, if you want the help of others to create that Future, you'll need to Engage them

That is, you will interact with them in a way that has them *wanting* to build the Future with you. Engagement is central to a leader's ability to build alignment, involvement, ownership, unity and team. Crucially, it is absolutely distinct from 'communicating to', 'presenting at', or 'telling'.

I am staggered that so many leaders still appear to believe that, in order to get the best from others, it's enough for them simply to 'transmit' their ideas or wishes. It isn't.

Engaging others is a two-way interaction and it's something that happens inside your relationships. To be fully effective, you'll need to engage people in yourself, as well as in the Future you want to create, and this calls for qualities like integrity, openness and consistency. When engagement occurs, not only is an enormous sense of possibility generated but people will be ready to knock down barriers as they pursue what they have helped to invent. What's possible for a group or organisation when people are really engaged can be immense.

And third, in Deliver, you make things happen

This is where words like 'performance, execution, implementation and results' live. Leading doesn't stop with 'vision' or 'team'. It ends with getting the best out of yourself and others in order to deliver results.

So when you are up to something, you start with ideas about what you'd like to see in the Future. Then you talk with others so they want to build it with you – you Engage them. Then you encourage and support them to make it happen, to Deliver. And if you're really being a leader rather than a doer, the other people you've engaged will make most of it happen.

Whatever the ambition or goal, this is what's involved: **Future–Engage–Deliver**. You'll notice I don't dwell on leadership competencies or qualities. Rather I prefer to focus you on what you have to get done, what you have to practise. If you want to be truly effective:

- you have to be guided by a Future you want,
- you have to Engage others, and
- you have to Deliver.

Let's get practical right now and start working with this framework by using it to look at your organisation and then you.

What do you see about your Organisation?

Have a look at your organisation through the *Future–Engage–Deliver* lens and consider these questions:

Future

● How strong is the sense of Future in your organisation? Is there an uplifting sense of purpose and ambition? Or is the focus more on analysing the past?

● Is there a sense of possibility in the air? Do people readily think about what could be achieved rather than what can't be done?

● Is there a feeling of optimism and hope? Is this strong enough to help people feel confident in the face of barriers?

Engage

● Are people engaged in and do they want to contribute to the goals of the organisation?

● Do they feel valued and involved?

● Do people look to engage colleagues or is it more a culture of 'communicate to and tell'?

Deliver

● Is your organisation strong at delivering what it sets out to?

● Are conversations about delivery full and robust, or do people 'go along' with what's being asked of them?

● Also, are people helped to develop in order to increase the organisation's overall capacity to deliver?

Ask the same questions about your department, team and key individuals. What do you see about how strong the leadership in your organisation is and where it's coming from?

What do you see about You?

Now let's turn to you. There is something here I really want you to take on board. It is that each of these aspects of leading requires what I call **Leadership Muscles** and the really good news is that you already have the Leadership Muscles for each of the three essential aspects of leading that I've outlined.

Let's demonstrate this now:

Future Muscles: At times, you have ideas about how you'd like things to be in the Future; you imagine, you dream, you visualise; you have ambitions and aspirations. This is the Leadership Muscle at the core of the Future aspect.

Engage Muscles: Similarly, there are times and places in your life where you've interacted with others so they've wanted to help you and do things for you. You already have the Muscles needed to Engage others.

Deliver Muscles: And finally, there have been times when you have followed up with people and they have delivered for you. This may have been delivery on a large or small scale. Either way, you were using your Deliver Muscles.

Not all your Muscles may be strong. That's ok – I've yet to work with a leader who's been really powerful in all three aspects of leading. Feel good about and exercise the Muscles that are strong, and enjoy developing through practice the ones that are weaker.

I'll show you how to do this as we go along and particularly in the next chapter where we'll look at how the leaders I've seen grow fastest do so.

> "We learn best when we are committed to taking charge of our own learning. Taking charge of our own learning is part of taking charge of our lives."
>
> Bennis and Goldsmith

In summary ...

Future–Engage–Deliver, it's as simple as that. Don't believe that this 'leadership stuff' is any more complicated whether you are leading a full organisation, a team or just yourself.

You already have all the fundamental Leadership Muscles. And you can grow each of them further with practice.

FED IN PRACTICE

RUTH MADDISON

Ruth Maddison is a headteacher in Nottinghamshire who has recently come across FED and is already in action. She writes:

'My husband recommended this book to me and when I picked it up I realised how useful and straightforward *Future–Engage–Deliver* is as a model for leadership and how easily it could be conveyed to others.

'First, the book has helped me recognise many areas where I can grow as a leader. I can so often be so busy with day-to-day concerns that I miss the real leadership that I can offer. I have certainly had to work on the Deliver Through Others agenda as I have found it hard to delegate. I recognised so much of me in that chapter and can also see where I have improved – another good thing that the book helps me to do.

'But best of all, the simplicity of the language means that I can quickly introduce leadership ideas to others. I have young staff who are being given leadership roles and need help in developing their skills. I also have very new staff who, as you say in the book, are also leaders and need to grow. All of us have begun to explore what it means to be At Our Very Best.

'All this, along with the growing of self-awareness and leadership skills in our pupils, has set me an exciting challenge – one that I'm keen to take on board wholeheartedly.'

How to turbo-charge your growth

... some people grow faster than others. You get to choose the pace.

- How to turbo-charge your growth
- **1** Make your practice Conscious Practice
- **2** Build your Support Team
- **3** Know and Go beyond Your Limits
  - Limit One: Not Believing You're a Leader
  - Limit Two: Not Being in Leader Mode

How to turbo-charge your growth

Some of the leaders I've worked with have grown in their confidence and ability a lot faster than others. This chapter will show you the approach to adopt if you want to grow at this accelerated pace. I've identified the three ways that you can turbo-charge your growth.

They are:

1 Make your practice **Conscious Practice**.

2 Build your personal **Support Team**.

3 Know and **Go beyond Your Limits**.

1 Make your practice Conscious Practice

The research on leadership is totally conclusive that you do most of your learning and growing as a leader in real-life situations, not on courses or reading books, and you grow fastest when you're taking on challenges that stretch you.

This is great news because it means you have the opportunity to practise, learn and grow your Leadership Muscles every day. You don't need to wait until that next leadership course; you can develop while you're doing what you're doing.

In this regard, improving as a leader is no different from improving in many walks of life such as playing an instrument or a sport – the more you practise the better you get. And the kind of practice that most accelerates learning and growth is Conscious Practice. That is, when you are consciously using situations and challenges as opportunities to learn and grow.

At its best, what this means is that you'll be conscious of how you want to be as a leader ahead of meetings, conversations or challenges; that you are aware of what's happening while you're in these situations, and are then pausing to extract learning afterwards. Even better, you'll be asking for feedback from others to learn even more.

Pause for a second now and check in on yourself:

- How clear are you that you have opportunities every day to practise being a leader?
- How regularly have you been grabbing those opportunities?
- What specific opportunities are coming up for Conscious Practice of your leadership?

The leaders I've seen grow fastest look out for these opportunities and what I'll do in this book is introduce you to some ideas that will help you extract more learning from your practice. These ideas will also help you identify which aspects of your leading you want to develop and how.

Through such Conscious Practice, you will build your confidence as a leader, want to take on bigger challenges and so grow your leadership even further.

> "What cannot be achieved by formula may be achieved by attention to the flow of Spirit and by continued practice. Effective leadership simply does not happen without practice."
>
> Harrison Owen

2 Build your Support Team

Ultimately, your leading is completely down to you. But do not try to grow fast as a leader all on your own.

If you want to grow fast, it's essential you create your personal Support Team.

Here's the first reason. When the impact of leadership development programmes in eight different organisations was studied, one of the main findings clearly highlighted the power of receiving regular feedback from colleagues. The study by Goldsmith and Morgan in 2004 found that:

> *'Leaders who discussed their own improvement priorities with their co-workers, and then regularly followed up with these co-workers, showed striking improvement.'*

'Leaders who did not have ongoing dialogue with colleagues showed improvement that barely exceeded random chance.'

It's as stark as that. So consider shifting your view from 'these are people I'm working with' to 'these are some of the people who can help me be a much more effective leader'.

If you really want to accelerate your growth, here's what to do. You identify the specific ways in which you want to grow as a leader; you tell selected colleagues and ask them to rate you in these areas now; you then ask them if they'll watch out for you in these areas because you'd like to talk to them regularly about what progress you're making. And do this whether you have a 360 degree feedback process in place or not.

This help from your Support Team can be the difference between *'striking improvement'* and *'improvement that barely exceeds random chance.'*

The second major reason to have a Support Team is that they can help in many other ways, too. We are all human. We all have setbacks, moments of doubt, times when we want to get stuff off our chests or just disappear and hide. With the help of others we can talk stuff through, get things back into perspective, have a laugh and re-energise ourselves.

So check in for yourself now:

- Do you have people you talk with who can help you get yourself back in shape?
- Who would you like on your Support Team who currently isn't there?
- What request will you make of people on your Support Team?

You already have people who help like this. But think wider. Who else could be on your Support Team? Who else could help you believe more in yourself and spend more time being at your best? You may not find asking for help easy, but for your rapid growth as a leader it's essential.

> "Leadership development can only occur in the tumult and possibilities of our relationships. Others help us see things we are missing, affirm whatever progress we have made, test our perceptions, and let us know how we are doing. They provide the context for experimentation and practice. Without others' involvement, lasting change can't occur."
>
> Daniel Goleman

FED IN PRACTICE

ORLA WHALLEY

Orla Whalley is a finance manager and mum of two. She wrote to us a while ago about her Support Team.

'It's easy to know when to go to your Support Team, right? When you need guidance, when you want some feedback on how you are being or just to check in and tell them how well you are doing.

'But what about when things aren't so great? I recently went through a period of ill health that left me absolutely physically drained. I got sick of myself in the end and I did something that seems completely backward to me now, I hid from my support network. It just felt wrong to own up to feeling like this in a culture of being "great", where how I was feeling might be seen as a personal weakness.

'It was only when one of my Support Team came looking for me that I realised I was trying to regroup on my own and to only contact people when I had "good" news. In that phone call, talking about how I really felt highlighted my mistake but also made me realise that it is sometimes hardest to use the support when we need it most.

'When I checked in with all the people who care about my emotional and physical wellbeing, without exception they came back to me with words of empathy, support and advice on how to keep going forwards. It was an

▶

eye-opener to realise that when I let people understand where I was at, I didn't get any sense of having become less of a person in their eyes.'

Orla finishes with some great questions: 'How often do you put a brave face on how you're feeling and not use your Support Team? And how ready are you to reach out to others who seem to be struggling?'

3 Know and Go beyond Your Limits

Put simply, there are two ways to grow as a leader. One is to build your Leadership Muscles with the help of Conscious Practice and your Support Team. The other is to notice and then reduce the ways in which you limit yourself.

In particular, there are two major ways that I've seen people limit themselves as leaders – and I can promise you that at least one applies to you! See how strong these limits are for you.

Limit One: Not Believing You're a Leader

The other day, I was asked to do a session on someone else's leadership programme. The group of 20 managers from this high-profile organisation were pleasant enough but there was no spark, no buzz. When we looked into this, we revealed that, even though they were on a leadership programme, most of them didn't see themselves as leaders!

What a waste of human potential. And this isn't an isolated case. I come across thousands of people who are held back just by the way they think about themselves and leadership. How has this come about?

My answer is that people have digested too much 'accepted wisdom' about leadership that is both out of date and seriously debilitating.

At its worst, this is how the story goes:

● Leaders are different from me; they are charismatic, probably heroic and perhaps even explorers!!

- In organisations, they are older and in senior positions; they may have been helped in getting there by going to the right school or university.

- These leaders have few doubts or insecurities. They are terrifically confident. They are somehow special.

- Also, to be good at this leadership stuff, we can be seduced into believing we'll have to understand complicated theories and models, and generally be pretty bright.

- Oh, and you'll also have to find the 'right' way to be a leader, the 'right' answer – how many years did I read books believing 'the answer' would be in the next one?

- And, finally, leadership is a solitary journey, one you must make alone.

Of course, this is a load of rubbish. But check in now to see whether you've been limiting your leadership potential by how you've been thinking about yourself. Consider these questions:

- What have you believed about 'leaders' and 'leadership'?
- What have you taken for granted and not stopped and really thought through?
- Who do you consider to be leaders, and who do you say are not?
- What do you believe it takes to be a leader?
- What are the characteristics you believe leaders must have?
- To what extent do you see yourself as a leader?

Overall, notice how strongly the way you think about leadership encourages you to see yourself as a leader and be a leader in your own right. You may be one of those not held back too much by this very common limit, in which case 'terrific'.

But if, like so many, you do have limiting beliefs around your own leadership, then simply notice them and go beyond them.

It's time instead to start focusing on who you want to be as a leader, what you're like when you're at your best and how you've been in those moments when you've been at your brilliant best.

Leading is a natural activity, a part of all of us, regardless of position, title, or place in the hierarchy. You already have the Leadership Muscles needed. You simply need to develop them through practice.

> "The illusion is obstinate and enduring: A mortal is seemingly anointed by the gods and is stamped with a unique gift that allows him or her to lead others. This person shines irrepressibly, and other mere mortals are compelled to follow. As prevalent as this notion is, it is demonstrably false, and any person who has seriously studied leadership has found that it is not a predetermined affair."
>
> Warren Bennis

Limit Two: Not Being in Leader Mode

I've little time for endless debates about whether leaders are made or born. A far more useful angle that can help people grow as leaders is the idea that at times we are in our **Leader Mode** – times when we are at our best and making things happen – and at times we are not.

Take Jane, for example. I worked with her when she was the successful Chief Executive of a division of a major company. She was then promoted into a prestigious global position.

Jane was a proven leader but, one afternoon when I met her, she certainly wasn't in her Leader Mode. Her energy was flat, she'd lost sight of her ambitions for her team and her business, and she was bogged down in detailed analyses of the past results.

Sadly, I've met thousands of people like Jane; people in leadership positions who've lost sight of themselves as leaders and have slipped back into what I call their **Operator/Manager Mode**, where their focus is on managing and doing, not leading.

I now believe that this characteristic is one of the major reasons why so many organisations perform way below what's possible.

What's going on here? This is what happens to some degree to all of us:

In our early days at work we succeed by becoming effective Operators. We fix this and sort that. We are then promoted and start to develop a strong Manager Mode, in which we supervise other Operators.

Before long, we each have a well-honed Operator/Manager Mode in which we feel both competent and comfortable, and which we know has been one of the reasons for our success to date.

In addition, although organisations are asking the Janes of this world to lead, they can also put them under relentless pressure to review the past and manage the present, rather than focus on the future.

And this isn't all. Many Janes do not grasp how fundamentally different it is to lead; so they can spend almost all their time in Operator/Manager Mode without realising it.

As a result, even people as capable as Jane can spend more time than they want to in Operator/Manager Mode. Of course, we all need to spend time in all three modes.

However, I have yet to find anyone who at times doesn't slide back into Operator/Manager when being in Leader Mode is what is needed.

So pause here to think about what you're like.

- What do you notice about the ways in which you spend your time?
- How clear are you about what you're like in your Operator/Manager and Leader Modes?
- What has you slide into Operator/Manager Mode when actually you don't want to?
- What do you notice about how your organisation encourages you to be in one mode or another?

Have no doubt, we all sometimes limit ourselves as leaders in this way, but happily there is something very simple we can do to know this limit and go beyond it.

It's Conscious Practice! Simply raise your awareness of the times and places you want to be in Leader Mode but have slipped into Operator/Manager Mode, and choose not to be.

This is how you do it:

- Remember some times when you've been in Leader Mode, when you've been at your best. How did you feel? How would you describe your energy? What were you doing? (If you struggle to recall some times, ask colleagues from your Support Team to give you examples.)

- Now list those times and places when you are in Operator/Manager Mode – in which meetings and interactions; on which projects; with who else in the room etc?

- In which of these situations do you want to be in Leader Mode?

- What's your picture of how you want to be at these times? Create a mental picture that has you feeling good and encourages you to be the leader you want to be. You can draw on the memories of when you've been in Leader Mode.

- Then, just ahead of these times, practise thinking about who you want to be.

- And then practise during these times being who you want to be.

This is one of the ways you can grow as a leader immediately. Some building of your Leadership Muscles may take time. But some of your practice can make a difference straight away. Have a stronger picture of you being the leader you want to be and simply practise being that leader in more situations, more of the time.

> "Leadership is often spoken of as if it were simply advanced management. The presumption is that whatever the manager is supposed to do, the leader does more of and better. Leadership is not advanced management; it is radically different from management, and to equate the two is to miss an essential distinction."
>
> Harrison Owen

In summary …

You can influence dramatically how fast you grow as a leader. You can flex and build your Muscles every day and you'll build them faster with the help of a Support Team. Also, be clear that you already have an effective Leader Mode. Get out there and practise it.

FED IN PRACTICE

THE MARKETING SOCIETY

Gemma Greaves is Marketing Director of The Marketing Society and was a participant on her own Society's leadership programme that we help run. Before then, she'd tell you that she was, '110% busy, had no time to think and there weren't enough hours in the day'.

The course was a real wake-up call for Gemma because she saw that she was deep in Operator/Manager Mode and not in her best Leader Mode. She was busy managing the present and doing little to imagine how she wanted the Society to grow and how great she wanted it to be. This all changed after the programme. She picks up the story:

'I sat listening to this leadership stuff thinking, "It all sounds great but I haven't the time to think about that!" But then the simplicity of FED pulled me in and I realised I wasn't doing Future and hadn't really worked out what we were building as a Society because I wasn't in Leader Mode.

'So the first thing I did after the programme was sit down with my Chief Executive, Hugh Burkitt, and agree our future vision. We established the positioning "Inspiring Bolder Marketing Leadership" and a new structure for our programme that now runs through everything we think and do. And we saw that we could take this message and expand our network globally. Already we have a presence in India with more countries to follow. These are definitely exciting times for The Marketing Society.

▶

'Personally, understanding my limiting beliefs and how to be where I want to be has been incredibly powerful both personally and professionally. Plus my team tells me I'm a better leader because together we have a clear vision and I'm giving them so much more room in which to grow and develop. Thank you, FED!'

Future–Engage–Deliver

. . . above anything else, leading is about being in touch with what you care about and then going for it.

- Future
  - Question 1 What do you care about?
  - Question 2 What do you want to lead for?
- Practices to build your Future Muscles
  - Be Guided by the Future you Want
  - Embrace the Big Picture, the Whole
- So why aren't we all already brilliant at leading?
- Future: How we Limit Ourselves
  - Question 3 Who is the Leader you want to be?

Future

In this chapter we'll make sure that the foundations of your leadership are in place. I will encourage you to create answers to three fundamental questions about your leadership and I will highlight specific practices which you can take on to build your Future Leadership Muscles.

Also, I'll help you identify how you limit yourself in the Future aspect of your leadership and how you can break through these limits.

Leading always starts in the Future. It always starts with ideas you have about what you'd like to see in the Future.

As I've already said, we all have the basic Leadership Muscle which allows us to imagine, dream or visualise what could be. For instance, you'll probably find it easy to dream about your next holiday or imagine something at work going really well. But when you're in your best Leader Mode there is another and immensely powerful factor at play. I want to draw your attention to this factor by telling you about Stephen, one of the most effective leaders I've worked with.

Interestingly, Stephen doesn't lead a team of people. He's never had more than a couple of direct reports, he's never run a main piece of the business and he's not on the executive team running this major corporation. Also, he wouldn't strike you instantly as inspirational and he couldn't tell you much about his psychometric profile.

However, there is something powerful in Stephen that I've found in every leader I've worked with – something that seems to be an essential ingredient of leadership and is more fundamental than anything to do with your title, position, personality or experience. It's this.

When you're in Leader Mode, like Stephen, you're 'up to something'. In other words you're in touch with something that's important to you and you're doing something about it.

This is what is so distinctive about the Future aspect of leading.

Leaders who are in touch with a Future that matters to them allow it to guide what they think and how they act every day.

Since I've known him, Stephen has always been 'up to something'; he's wanted his company to succeed. He didn't report to Richard, the Chief Executive, but he would regularly give Richard feedback about what he saw in the company that was and wasn't working. And if he wasn't meeting Richard, he would send him a personal letter to give him his feedback instead.

Not surprisingly, Richard began to value this truthful input so he invited Stephen to help facilitate his team meetings and give feedback on what he saw. Richard will tell you that, over the next couple of years, Stephen made a material difference to the ambition, culture and performance of the company – exactly what Stephen was 'up to' and wanted to make happen.

I know that, at times, you're just like Stephen. When you're in your best Leader Mode you don't have just any ideas about what you want to see in the Future. You have ideas directly linked to what you care about. And this is what gives you your drive and ambition and inspires you to take action.

Of course, being a leader who is 'up to something' doesn't guarantee that progress will be straightforward and easy. You'll meet resistance and apathy; you'll suffer setbacks and disappointments; you may have moments when you think about giving up. So why do you keep going? Because what you're up to matters to you. You care.

If there is only one idea you take from this book, my request is that you make it this one. Leadership is not about your competencies, skills and personality. It's first and foremost about being in touch with what you care about and then going for it.

There are other people who emphasise this critical point, too. Here's how they put it:

'In the corporate world there is so much pressure to say yes, even if we are only halfway there. Disapproval from the wrong quarter can be deadly for prospects and advancement. Yes or no, the voice throws us back on what we want for our life. It forces us to ask ourselves Who is speaking? Who came to work today? Who is working for what? What do I really care about?'

DAVID WHYTE, author and poet

'We can create the lives and organisations we desire only by understanding the enlivening spirit in us that always is seeking to express itself.'

MARGARET WHEATLEY, President, Berkana Institute

'So the "how-to" books and the "great-men" books give people a formula that is missing the most critical ingredient that the great people had, which was they took a stand for something and did what ever had to happen.'

RICHARD PASCALE, Associate Fellow, Oxford University

I'm putting particular emphasis on this point because I'm not confident that you'll have been told this. I say this because every month I meet people wanting useful tools and techniques about leadership. But when I probe we quickly uncover that they are not in touch with what they care about, they haven't realised that this is where it all starts and so they don't have that energising feeling of being 'up to something'.

To make this real for you, I believe you need to answer two essential leadership questions. You'll be a more effective leader more of the time if you can quickly connect with your answers to these questions. These are usually among the first questions I ask all the leaders I work with.

Question 1 What do you care about?

Other ways to reflect on this question are to ask yourself what matters to you, what's important to you, what you value most or what you have most passion for.

This is where your leadership starts. You won't be a great leader for things you don't care about! You can be for what you do care about.

There is, of course, no one right way to answer this question or one right answer. And there are many different aspects of your life you might want to think about. Here are a few that might just prompt your thinking …

the planet,
family, work, friends, values,
goals, relationships, purpose,
quality of life, security,
money, ambitions,
health …

As soon as you can, go and find some quiet time and start scribbling down your first ideas about what you care about

_____

_____

_____

_____

_____

_____

_____

_____

When you have had a go at this, there is something I want you to notice. How are you feeling? How is your energy? If you are not full of life and feeling good, you've not got to your answer.

Be clear, this is not an intellectual exercise. This is about connecting with *'the enlivening spirit in us that always is seeking to express itself'*. It's about tapping into your energy of passion, pride and possibility.

You may get in touch with this energy faster if you talk out loud to someone. Consider asking someone in your Support Team to sit you down and ask you questions like:

> *Ok, so tell me what matters to you.*
> *What's important in your life?*
> *What do you care about?*
> *What matters deeply to you?*

If you're still struggling, go ahead a few pages to read about how we limit ourselves in imagining the Future; this may free you up. And, if then you're still stuck, get in touch with us and we'll see if we can help.

Answering this question and feeling good and energised by your answer then prepares you to answer the next question to further develop your leadership.

> "To laugh often and much; to win the respect of intelligent people and the affection of children; to earn the appreciation of honest critics and endure the betrayal of false friends; to appreciate beauty, to find the best in others; to leave the world a little better; whether by a healthy child, a garden patch or a redeemed social condition; to know even one life has breathed easier because you have lived. This is the meaning of success."
>
> Ralph Waldo Emerson

Question 2 What do you want to lead for?

The job here is to link 'what you care about' to what is real, tangible and specific. So, what do you want to actually make happen in the Future you want?

There are various ways to get into this question. For example, what do you want to take action on? What results do you want to achieve? What specifically do you want to make happen that is part of what you care about?

I summarise all of these in the question 'What do you want to lead for?' and I encourage you to think about what you want to lead for in terms of your organisation, your colleagues, your customers and anywhere else in life where you have the opportunity to make a difference.

Again, notice your energy after you've answered this question. If there's any sense of 'I *should* lead for this' then beware. This isn't about settling for someone else's agenda or doing something dutifully. Rather it's about being aligned with what matters to you and it's you who gets to choose.

_____

_____

_____

_____

_____

_____

_____

When you've answered these questions, I invite you to flex your Future Muscles now. Imagine what could be next for you, now you are in touch with what you care about and what you want to lead for. Here are some questions to stimulate you:

- What could you do next to further what you care about?
- What new conversations could you have – and with whom – about what you want to see happen?
- What's happening in your life that you will simply stop tolerating and do something about?
- In which situations could you switch from Operator/Manager Mode to Leader Mode and what new opportunities might appear?

My hope for you is that in addressing these questions you will open up all sorts of new possibilities for you as a leader. But now is the time I also want to emphasise an important insight I want you to see about yourself:

There are times when you have already been the leader you want to be, bringing into the world what it is you care about, making real what you want to lead for.

That is, being a leader is already a part of you; you already have an effective Leader Mode. The question is not 'Will I ever be a leader when I get old enough or at a senior enough level?' It's more about how you can grow even faster as a leader to make even more of a difference to what matters to you now.

And the way you do this is by building your Leadership Muscles through Conscious Practice. Here's how.

> "As I look back I note that most of the things I was trying to say revolved around the small cluster of basics that have resonated with me for most of my adult life. To communicate as an authentic leader, you have to look into your own experience and find those themes that are most important to you."
>
> Derek Walcott

FED IN PRACTICE

DAVID MADDISON

Like all headteachers, David Maddison is being challenged to develop himself and his staff as leaders. However, David has inspired us by using FED to also help develop his primary school children as leaders!

He writes, 'You know that FED has helped us as teachers wonderfully to have different conversations with each other. Well, FED is also helping us to open up discussions with children around leadership and develop their early understanding of what it is to lead.

'We want the challenges we're offering our pupils to engage and involve them in learning in a way that they will enjoy, be positively affected by and remember. As part of this, we are moving from talking with pupils about what their "learning objectives" need to be to having a conversation with them about what we are up to and asking them: "What are you Up2?"

'We're having more conversations with pupils about their futures, building on what they are Up2 now, and how we can help them explore what they'd like to get Up2 in their lives. All of this is part of inspiring them and engaging them and having them go for (Go4) it.

'For the kids, this is such cool language. Up2, Go4 – it's definitely got a chance! We are also about to experiment with giving children an "Up2 Book" which will be personal to them (i.e. not marked by teachers) in which they can keep their own ideas, personal thoughts, notes, etc. All part of emphasising the concept and importance of future-focused leading, goal-driven living and knowing the direction you are travelling in.

'Even children can be up to something. What are you Up2 and what are you Going4? And if you haven't already got a leadership journal, how about getting your own Up2 Book?'

Practices to build your Future Muscles

When you're in touch with what you care about and what you want to lead for, the core foundations of your leadership are in place. But how can these foundations influence your leadership each day? The short answer is by consciously taking on two practices that I have seen effective leaders excel at.

1 Be Guided by the Future you Want

I'll always remember a phone call with an HR Director, Nic, about his latest staff survey results. He told me that he was pleased to see that the score on one factor had moved up from 30 to 37 per cent. 'That sounds good,' I said, 'and ideally what would you like the score to be?' 'Oh, 80 per cent,' he replied, instantly seeing the result in a new light.

Nic had done what we all tend to do; he'd viewed the present from the past. He was comparing where the company had got to with where they'd come from – it's a common practice of Operator/Managers. In Leader Mode, however, we view the present through a different lens; we compare where we are with where we want to be.

As someone once said, 'It's not what a vision is; it's what a vision does.' That is, what matters is what it 'does' at this very moment now to guide your focus and thinking. Your ideas about the Future you want give you a powerful lens through which to look at current reality. This lens influences what you see and pay attention to. It helps you to focus on what matters. It helps you see what is working and what may be missing that you'll need to put in place.

To make sure that you are being Guided by the Future you Want rather than the present or the past, practise asking yourself the following questions:

● How does what exists now compare with how I want things to be?

● What's the size of the gap between where things are and where I want them to be?

● What's missing from today that I want to see in the Future?

● On what fronts must I work in order to move fastest to the Future I want?

● What must I attend to today to move to where I want to be?

Yes, make sure to acknowledge progress from the past – the score did move from 30 to 37 per cent. But questions like these will help to ensure you never lose sight of your dream, your aspiration, your equivalent of the 80 per cent score that you are looking for.

> "The goal of Strategic Intent is to fold the future back into the present. The important question is not 'How will next year be different from this year?' but 'What must we do differently next year to get closer to our Strategic Intent?'"
>
> Hamel and Prahalad

2 Embrace the Big Picture, the Whole

I've facilitated many team meetings in different parts of the world and I've often asked myself the question, 'If I didn't know who the hierarchical leader in this room was, how would I work it out?' The answer started to dawn on me a few years ago. I began to see that the leader was not necessarily the brightest person in the room, as some of my old thinking about leadership led me to believe. What I saw was that often the leader was the most practised at taking a couple of steps back from the content and looking at the bigger picture, the context.

Being a master of context involves being able to see not whether we are climbing the ladder successfully but whether it's leaning against the right wall!

At times, this will include seeing how this project or goal fits in with other priorities or other activities elsewhere in the organisation. Or how it compares with what others in the field are up to. Or what customers are saying they really want. Or where society and technology trends are headed.

So the second practice that will build your Future Leadership Muscles is to keep revisiting the bigger picture, the context, in order that you can speak to not just the 'what' is needed by 'when' but also 'why' it is needed at all.

This is a considerable shift from our learned behaviour as Operators and Managers when we developed the ability to focus on a part of the whole, a task or a short-term goal. In Leader Mode we need to be able to see the whole as well as the parts. And, if you've answered the questions earlier in this chapter, you will have already flexed this Muscle.

Notice I didn't ask you in those questions what you wanted to achieve on a short-term task, project or challenge you have. I first asked you to step back and get in touch with the whole of what you care about, the context that will shape your leadership.

Similarly, you can practise building this muscle each day by answering those questions that get you in touch with the bigger picture, such as:

- Let's remind myself, why am I doing this?
- How does what I'm working on connect with what I care about and am leading for?
- What is the bigger whole that what I'm working on is a part of?

These can be particularly valuable questions at times of difficulty. One of our most powerful ways of bouncing back from setbacks, upsets and disappointments is to pause and get back in touch with what we care about and why we are doing what we're doing. It's so easy to lose sight of this picture in the hurly burly of everyday life.

To demonstrate some of the power of putting both of these practices into action, let me tell you about a dot com business I've worked with. The team in question had been pleased with their healthy rate of growth, until they stepped back and properly looked at the bigger picture of technology and customer trends, the rate of competition growth and where the world could be in three to five years' time. It was only then that they saw that they'd need to move much faster, build new alliances and turn lots of their thinking on its head, in order to have the winning Future they wanted. By shifting their context they are now being guided by a much clearer picture of the Future they Want and are moving there at a dramatically faster rate.

> "The ability to maintain perspective in the midst of action is critical. We call this skill 'getting off the dance floor and going to the balcony', an image that captures stepping back from the action and asking, 'What's really going on here?'"
>
> Heifitz and Linsky

So why aren't we all already brilliant at leading?

There is something I notice about everyone I work with. As well as having our own unmistakable talents and magic, we also have our limits. And what distinguishes the fastest-growing leaders is that they have not only exercised their strengths, they have also consistently sought to go beyond their limits.

In this book, as well as helping you to build your Leadership Muscles I also want to help you see how you too limit yourself as a leader and so give you the best chance to go beyond those limits. I outline the most common ways in which I see people limiting themselves in the chapters on each of the Future, Engage and Deliver practices of leading. At times, it's working on your limits that'll give you the greatest progress in your development.

Future: How we Limit Ourselves

You could say that being good at the Future aspect of leading is just about imagining and having ideas about what you want. And you'd be right, it is simple – but I have seen three very common ways in which people limit themselves and their Future.

1 **_Thinking from the Present._** I have flagged this issue a number of times already. The pull of the present can be overwhelming. The immediacy of what's happening now can have us lose sight of the big picture and where we want to be. There isn't one leader I've worked with who hasn't from time to time got sucked into the detail and slipped back into Operator/ Manager Mode unknowingly – it's human! The key here is to be conscious. Ask yourself, 'Am I thinking from the present or past, or am I being Guided by the Future I Want?'

2 **_'I can't see How'._** One of the most effective ways we have of limiting ourselves in life is not to take things on because we don't know ahead of time how we are going to do them. However, this 'not knowing' doesn't hold you back when you're in Leader Mode. When you're 'up to something' you rarely know exactly how you're going to make it happen. You simply want to make it so and you get on with it. This is the power of commitment. Think of all the things you've achieved in life that you didn't know how to do when you started but you were determined you'd succeed. Take walking and riding a bike as prime examples!

> "Until one is committed there is hesitancy, the chance to draw back – always ineffectiveness. Concerning all acts of initiative there is one elementary truth, the ignorance of which kills countless ideas and splendid plans: That the moment one definitely commits oneself, then Providence moves too."
>
> W H Murray

3 **_Our Limiting Beliefs._** And now for the most powerful way we limit ourselves. If we really want to be at our best more of the time this is a topic we really need to explore. So let's start here and then go into more depth later in Chapter 7.

I'll move into this topic by telling you a bit more about my own journey. I used to think it was only me who was plagued with self-doubt and who questioned whether I was really good enough or smart enough to do the jobs I was doing.

It seemed to me that everyone else appeared to be confident while I was worrying about whether I'd be found out!

Over the years I have learned that this is a totally false picture. Through honest conversations with many impressive people I have come to realise that all of us have doubts, fears and uncertainties – and that at times these beliefs and feelings seriously hold us back.

If you met me today you'd probably think that I'm a confident sort of guy. So you'd likely be surprised to know that from time to time I'm thinking, 'What am I doing here? I'm just a lad from Wigan!'

Such thinking is an example of our Limiting Beliefs – and, while you may not share the same ones that I have, be in no doubt that you have your own set of Limiting Beliefs that sometimes will hold you back from being who you want to be. Common Limiting Beliefs that many people have shared with me include:

I'm too young   I'm too old

I'm only …   I'm not bright enough

I can't do it

I'm not worthy of more   I'm just …

I'm just not good enough

I don't have a degree

Which of these strikes a chord with you? The message I want to underline here is that such beliefs can seriously work against you flexing your Future Muscles. When I've worked with people struggling to tell me about the Future they'd really like, I've invariably found that they are held back for reasons linked to their Limiting Beliefs. For instance, some people don't see how they deserve any more than they've currently got – I can relate to that one. Others won't allow themselves to think about what they really want because they don't believe they could make it happen, so why set themselves up for failure?

I've explored the power of Limiting Beliefs with thousands of people and I have some good news and some bad news! The bad news is that they don't go away. The good news is that there is a lot you can do to loosen their grip on you. Here's what you do.

First, practise being conscious of them. The power of Limiting Beliefs often fades rapidly when we're aware of them and name them. So if I catch myself feeling powerless and not in Leader Mode, I'll ask myself what I'm thinking and feeling. For me, it will often be something linked to, *'I'm just a lad from Wigan'* or *'I'm not good enough'*. Recognising this gives me the chance to see if I really do believe these notions. Most of the time, I don't really. It's as if these Limiting Beliefs have been asleep and they've been wakened by something or someone and they're now controlling how I'm feeling and behaving.

So for now …

- Think of some times when you feel powerless, trapped or just ineffective. Then ask yourself what you're believing about yourself in such moments.
- Check in and ask yourself how much you really really believe that these ideas are really true.
- Smile.
- And then connect with your answer to the next key question for anyone growing themselves as a leader.

"Most of us hold one of two contradictory beliefs that limit our ability to create what we want. The more common is belief in our powerlessness – our inability to bring into being all the things we really care about. The other belief centres on unworthiness – that we do not deserve to have what we truly desire."

Peter Senge

Question 3 Who is the Leader you want to be?

On your journey as a leader you will have setbacks and disappointments that knock your energy and confidence. You will have moments when it'll feel that your Limiting Beliefs are true. What I strongly recommend you turn to at these times is a description of what you're like at your best, when you're being just who you want to be. This way you can give yourself a moment to choose who you want to be.

Let me tell you about the first time I practised this consciously a few years ago. At that time, about 80 per cent of my work was in one global company and I was helping to stimulate a powerful culture change across many of its operations. Then, one Tuesday, I got a call from a director, saying, 'Steve, I think you should know, I've just been in a meeting with the Chairman and he's said, "I am not having Steve Radcliffe run this company".' Oh dear!

On Friday, I was having lunch with this Chairman and, as I was about to step into the meeting room, the HR director grabbed me to say that the Chairman was in a foul mood and he'd forgotten I was coming for lunch. As you can imagine, my Limiting Beliefs seemed at that moment very real! I was feeling quite afraid and was ready to run home. But instead I took a quiet moment and asked myself who I wanted to be. My answer was that I wanted to be an expert consultant making a positive difference to the lives of thousands of people in this organisation.

So I took a deep breath, swapped greetings with the Chairman, and dived straight in. I asked him to tell me if I was causing him any nuisance through the work we were doing. We talked it through, everything was sorted and I continued to help him and his leadership team to create a new, vibrant culture throughout the organisation. I had been who I'd wanted to be.

It isn't always easy, but it's always possible for you to ask the same question I asked myself. Who is the leader you want to be?

You need to have an energising answer to the question and my request to you is to write down your response here and now. Don't hold back. There's no room for modesty here or playing safe because your Limiting Beliefs are talking quietly to you. Flex your Future Muscles and picture the Future when you're being at your very best, being the leader you want to be.

The leader I want to be is

_____

_____

_____

_____

_____

_____

_____

_____

When you've answered this question, notice your energy and recognise how you're feeling. This knowledge of who you want to be is something to remember and use. When things aren't going well or you're not on form, pause; get in touch with how you want to be and get energised by the prospect.

Imagine if you were that way now, what you would do, how you would feel, how you would speak. Allow yourself to be uplifted by being connected to who you are when you're at your best.

This is one of the most powerful practices I can suggest to you. You'll create more of the Future you want when you're being the leader you want to be. And I believe this is such an important practice that I have more to say on this topic later in Chapter 7. When you've finished this chapter, feel free to go there if you want to and then come back to the next chapter on Engage.

> "Becoming a leader is an individual process and means a deep awareness of who we are and the sort of human being we want to become. Once we know this, it can be expressed in our relationships and actions at work."
>
> Hilarie Owen

In summary ...

We have started at the foundations of your leadership. Everything else sits on top of your answers to the big three questions in this chapter:

1 What do you care about?

2 What do you want to lead for?

3 Who is the Leader you want to be?

Being clear on what you care about, what you're leading for and who you want to be as a leader will give you clarity and the strength to bounce back in times of difficulty.

And watch out for those Limiting Beliefs. They cause all sorts of mischief if you let them!

IN PRACTICE

STEVE HOLLIDAY

Steve Holliday has been practising being the leader he wants to be in his role in Siemens. He writes,

'I was heading south on the train last night from Newcastle, having just met a number of new colleagues. I felt exhilarated that we had built relationships way more than I'd hoped for. And I reflected on how this had happened.

'Before my meetings, my energy had been bouncing between excitement about what I hoped to achieve, mixed with some anxiety about the unknown and how it might go. I had wondered whether they would like me, whether I would show up at my best and whether I was good enough! Playing with such feelings and thoughts helped me reconnect with who I am when I'm at my best and it was then this simple – I went for it – without knowing the end result, but guided by a future I'm passionate about.

'This reflection also meant that when I met my new colleagues I was listening well and paying attention to them while staying true to what I stood for and believed in. This sense of exploring possibility felt rather like the start of a voyage where, despite the uncertainties ahead, we were able to generate an early sense of confidence, belief and commitment.

'As I passed Sheffield, I shared my feelings with my friend, Martin, and his response made me smile. He asked, "Why isn't it like this all the time? It's effortless."

'My answer is that it can be more of the time if we choose it. But in order for that to occur we have to pay real attention to ourselves, our relationships and the exciting futures we're passionate about. And while we may not always get it right, it becomes so much more likely when we're ready every day to practise showing up as the leader we want to be.'

Future–**Engage**–Deliver

Engage is fundamentally different to 'communicate at' or 'tell' and not enough people get this.

- Future–**Engage**–Deliver
- 'Engage', different from 'Future'
- Levels of Engagement
- Engagement: What's involved
- The Relationship to Results Pyramid
- The Four Aspects of Engagement
  - **1** Relationships
  - **2** Possibilities, Ideas
  - **3** Opportunities, Priorities
  - **4** Actions
- Three 'Engage' Practices
  - **1** Consciously Practise 'Engaging' rather than 'Transmitting/Communicating'
  - **2** Consciously Practise Building Big Relationships
  - **3** Consciously Manage your 'Shadow of a Leader'

Future–Engage–Deliver

In this chapter, I'll help you see how Engage adds power to the Future aspect of leading, what the key ingredients of effective engagement are, and what practices you can take on to be a significantly more engaging leader.

Tim is the head of a high-profile organisation where he leads tens of thousands of people. And he's a world-class example of how *not* to engage people! I'll bet you know a few people like Tim.

Yes, Tim is clear on what he wants to lead for but his predominant style is to 'transmit' and 'tell', rather than 'connect' with people and 'engage' them. People around him feel talked at and at times talked down to. It's as if he simply expects people to obey. And, although people go along with a lot of what he wants, crucially Tim does not leave people *wanting* to bring their very best and *wanting* to go that extra mile.

In contrast to this situation, I often see the magic of what's possible when people are truly engaged. So I continue to be amazed that I regularly come across 'Tims' who are miles away from tapping into the brilliance of the people around them.

So my encouragement to you is not simply to 'transmit', 'present', 'report' or 'tell' but look to 'engage' people so they want to work with you and build a Future with you. This is how you add pace and velocity to what you're leading for.

> "All of the winning leaders I've studied share a passion for people. They also know how to keep themselves engaged in what they are doing at the moment. Leaders focus on how they make people feel after each interaction."
>
> Noel Tichy

'Engage', different from 'Future'

The Future piece of leading focuses on you. It's about your thinking, your imagining and getting clear on what you care about. In Future, your awareness is on yourself, how your spirits are and you choosing to be in Leader Mode. You can actually do great work in Future without needing contact with anyone else.

Engage is different. Engage is about your impact on others, how you connect with them, how you stimulate their thinking and impact their energy. You still need self-awareness but in Engage you must also be aware of the situation and how people are behaving and feeling around you. This is the 'emotional intelligence' territory.

Another way to think about Engage is to recognise that it always happens inside your relationships with others. So much of your ability to engage others lies in your ability to build big, strong relationships that help you get the job done.

When I'm talking about Big Relationships I'm not talking about you liking everyone and everyone liking you. I'm pointing to the sort of relationships you already have that you might call strong, easy or healthy ... relationships that really help you work together and get stuff done.

You could say that in your Big Relationships, people are not engaged just in the work you do together, they are also engaged in you.

This is an important distinction – because when you're looking to engage people to work with you, the best results will come when they are choosing to engage both in the Future you want to build together and in you. You know this from your own experience. Think about times when you've been truly engaged by another, and notice that while you've been engaging in the Future goal or project you've also been engaging in them.

Let's go back to Tim and see how he was seriously limiting himself as a leader. Here was a man who was very bright with bags of Intellectual Energy to bring to the Future aspect of leading. But he was low on Emotional Energy, the energy of human relationships. And even worse, he believed that in order to have people follow him it would simply be a case of bringing more Intellectual Energy – more logic, more analysis, more argument.

Please note I'm not saying you have to be a certain sort of inspirational or charismatic person. What I'm saying is that there is a job to be done in your interactions with others if you want to have the Future you want. To one extent or another, you will be engaging people around you. I'm encouraging you to be conscious of this job to be done and do it as best you can, whatever your personality or other traits.

One of the ways in which I helped Tim with his engagement was to help him discover what impact he was having on his colleagues. He learned about this by asking them for feedback and he was surprised to find that there was a big gap between the impact he wanted to have, his **Impact Intended**, and the impact he actually had, his **Impact Felt**. With this information, he was able to see that he needed to engage people differently to help them want to bring their very best. This was the start of a dramatic shift in Tim's effectiveness as a leader.

But before we look at how you can be even more engaging, I want to be absolutely clear about the benefits that come from people being engaged. There are a couple of models I use for these topics. You can download them from **www.futureengagedeliver.com/book.**

Levels of Engagement

In the Engage leg of leading, there are two particular aspects to pay attention to. First, there is of course the Future you want expressed as a goal, strategy or plan. Second, and at times more importantly, there is also how people are relating to that goal or plan. If your leading includes too much 'transmit' or 'tell', you may not notice where people are and how they are relating to what you want. On the other hand, if your intention is to engage people, you'll pay close attention to this matter.

So what will you do if others don't care how inspiring your vision is, or how compelling your strategy is? What if they resist what you want? The following model, adapted from Peter Senge's 'Possible attitudes toward a vision' (Senge 1993), gives you a way of thinking about where they might be in relation to the Future you are leading for as well as providing you with some powerful insights about how to engage them.

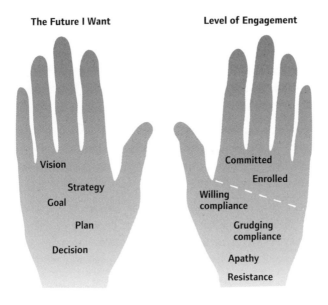

The Future I Want

Vision
Strategy
Goal
Plan
Decision

Level of Engagement

Committed
Enrolled
Willing
compliance
Grudging
compliance
Apathy
Resistance

On the left-hand side of this model you will see listed various aspects of the Future you may be leading for. On the right-hand side are some terms that describe the ways that people might be relating to, or are engaged with, that Future. And it is this right-hand side that I now want to examine.

Starting at the bottom right of the model, you'll see the word **Resistance**. Here people don't want what you want and they'll resist. They may put down what you're about, or engage colleagues in going a different way. Either way, you certainly won't get a lot of pace from them while they stay here.

At the next level up, some people simply may not care about what you're up to, they are in **Apathy**. People in this space can be the most difficult to engage and shift.

At a slightly more positive level, some people may be in **Grudging compliance**. There's a sense here of, 'Well, I wouldn't do that, but if that's what you want me to do, ok. But I'm only doing it because I have to, not because I agree with it.' Here you get some traction, but there's also a distinct dragging of feet.

One step up from here is **Willing compliance**, the territory of 'good soldiers'. Here, people will take actions in line with the vision, strategy, plan. There's a sense of, 'Ok, if that's what you want, I'll get on with it,' but there is no burning enthusiasm. There's a lot that can be achieved by people in **Willing compliance**. This Level of Engagement can be enough to have 'business as usual' run pretty well.

At the levels I've highlighted so far, people are at best 'going along with' what you want. But the real magic occurs when people *choose* to join you, when they want what it is you want and naturally bring their creativity, enthusiasm and ideas. Here, they are **Enrolled**.

But even when people are Enrolled, they can be distracted and they may switch to other priorities. This all changes when the people you engage get **Committed** to what you're up to. Now they bring their own energy because what they care about is touched and they really do want what you want.

I use this model a lot with clients. It really helps prompt a conversation about how engaged people are and how engaged a leader wants them to be. Let's use the model now to look at what you're like and what's happening around you. First, notice for yourself:

● What in life and work are you resistant to or apathetic about? What priorities that others see as important do you not want to put any energy into? If you look, you'll see things at home and at work.

● What in life and work do you 'go along with'? What do others want to see or make happen that you comply with but don't bring anything extra to? (To this question, I always think about jobs round the house!)

● What in life and work have you chosen to participate in and make happen? In what are you engaged, i.e. Enrolled or Committed?

● How are your energy and attitude different when you are engaged?

● What extra is possible because you're engaged? What can happen faster?

Most people say that they are very different when they are engaged versus 'going along with' or not caring. I want you in touch with how you are different so you can imagine just how different your team, project or organisation could be if most of its people were truly engaged.

Now, how would you say that people in your organisation relate to its vision, mission or goals? What are some of the priorities in your organisation that people are generally not committed to? How well do you see your organisation's leaders 'engaging' people? And just how different would the place be if people were engaged and bringing their very best to work each day? What could happen that doesn't seem possible today?

You may work in an organisation with high levels of engagement. Unfortunately, you are in the minority. Surveys galore regularly quantify low levels of engagement in organisations the world over and this fits with what I have seen on my travels.

Now take a moment to consider where people you work with are in relation to what you are up to. Can you identify those who are engaged and those who are not? What do you notice about how much easier it is working with those who are engaged? How much does work happen faster?

Part of my ambition here is to help you think much more about consciously engaging others and building your Engage Leadership Muscles. To that end, let's now look at what's involved in engaging others, and how you can become even more effective at it.

> "Full engagement begins with feeling eager to work in the morning and equally happy to return home in the evening. It means being able to immerse yourself in the mission you are on, whether that is grappling with a creative challenge at work, spending time with loved ones or simply having fun. Full engagement implies a fundamental shift in the way we live our lives."
>
> Loehr and Schwartz

Engagement: What's involved

Again, let me restate that this is not completely new territory for you. There are already times you are engaging and do engage others. Also, you already know quite a bit about what's involved in making engagement happen. I know this because I've asked thousands of people to help identify the key ingredients of engagement and I've never been met with silence!

Demonstrate this to yourself now by thinking about someone who you would say is engaging. Alternatively, identify how you are when you're engaging or think of a time when you've been engaged by someone. What were some of the ingredients present when engagement happened? Before reading on, note down your first thoughts here:

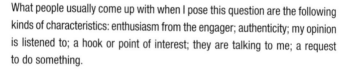

What people usually come up with when I pose this question are the following kinds of characteristics: enthusiasm from the engager; authenticity; my opinion is listened to; a hook or point of interest; they are talking to me; a request to do something.

There isn't a definitive list because leaders engage people differently and people get engaged differently, but happily I've seen it's possible to group all the possible ingredients under just four headings. I believe you'll need to pay attention to these if you're going to be great at engaging others.

The Relationship to Results Pyramid

Here is my all-time favourite model inside the *Future–Engage–Deliver* framework. At some time, I'll use it with every client because it's so quick to reveal what's happening in any interaction with either an individual or group. When things aren't working for you as a leader, it quickly points to why that is and what you can do about it. If there were one model I'd want to influence how you read situations, meetings and any other interactions, this would be the one. It will help you in many ways, including how to be a more engaging leader.

Basically, to get things done, we first generate **Possibilities and Ideas** of what could be. We then choose certain **Opportunities and Priorities** that we'll plan and focus on. And then we'll take **Actions** inside those Opportunities. And this leads to **Results**. It looks like this:

There's no rocket science here, but there is real value in you being able to separate the different aspects to making Results happen. However, although this all looks simple and straightforward, the problem is that human beings are involved! And all the work that goes on inside this pyramid happens inside our **Relationships**. So the full Pyramid is this:

There is a very good reason why the shape of the model is a Pyramid – and I'd really like to shout it from the rooftops:

You have to have Relationships big enough to get the job done.

Remember, by 'big enough' I mean 'strong enough' or 'good enough'.

I am in this territory every month when I'm with leaders who've done a great job on vision, strategy, budgets or plans but aren't getting traction because people aren't engaged. What's missing is so clear – they haven't got Relationships big enough for people to be engaged and want to move forward with them. Remember Tim? He had been a classic example of this kind of leader and the Pyramid for him looked like this:

Results

Actions

Opportunities, Priorities

Possibilities, Ideas

Relationships

As you can see, in Tim's world there is much in place. There is no shortage of Possibilities. Priorities have been identified and the desired Action is clear. But the Relationships Tim typically has with people are small and so they hold back from being truly engaged by him.

And Tim is not alone. Many leaders I come across in all walks of life are limiting themselves and their ambitions by not attending to this crucial aspect of leading – the size and nature of their Relationships.

I want to be really clear here to anyone searching for the tips and techniques of leadership or the processes involved. The Future aspect of leadership is about who you are being when you are alive with a sense of a Future you want. The Engage aspect is about how you show up in your Relationships.

That is, leadership is about what you're like and how you come across, not what techniques you've got to bring to the party or what processes you want to put in place.

Your influence and impact on others comes via your Relationships. These are the channels through which you lead others, engage others and have them want to walk with you. They have to be big enough to get the job done.

I'm going to reinforce this message in different ways but for now I want to help you use the Pyramid to see what's central to effective engagement and how you can up your game.

> "Leadership is a relationship. It's a relationship between those who aspire to lead and those who choose to follow. Sometimes, the relationship is one to one. Sometimes, it's one to many. Regardless of the number, leaders must master the dynamics of this relationship."
> Jim Kouzes

FED IN PRACTICE

JOHN HARPER

A few years ago when John Harper became UK Managing Director of Hasbro, one of the two global toy companies, things were in pretty bad shape. The four UK businesses were losing money, morale and confidence were at an all-time low, and customer service was non-existent.

John needed to move quickly to get the business back into financial health and re-energise the people, and this would be made doubly difficult by a significant and unavoidable downsizing.

John had become a big fan of FED earlier in his career and he knew that this was the time to be bold in his leadership. His brief to me was clear. He wanted his teams to connect to three big FED ideas:

1 What is the Future we want and how great can we be?

2 How do we Play to Win and perform At Our Best?

3 How do we build our Relationships internally and with customers so we can deliver the future together as a team?

To get started, John closed the companies for a day and brought everyone together to start exploring these ideas. We had a truly transformational day. People spoke the truth about how things had been and how they felt, and then went on to co-invent the future they wanted, with new stronger relationships as the foundation.

From that day on, it was John's leadership and the leadership he sparked in others that turned the company round. He's now running a great Hasbro business across Europe and says, 'Re-energising the UK business was such a rewarding time. We transformed customer service levels, profitability and morale. It's simple, really. Imagine a great future. Liberate the people. Build great relationships.'

The Four Aspects of Engagement

I have guided hundreds of leaders on ways they can be more engaging in their one-on-one conversations, with teams or in larger groups. When people have been engaged, ingredients in each of the four boxes of the Pyramid leading to Results have been present. Let's identify what's involved at each level.

1 Relationships

The idea of 'engaging' is getting more press these days but more leaders are talking about 'engaging' rather than being 'engaging'. What most of them haven't grasped – or are avoiding – is that engagement only happens in a particular kind of relationship.

The truth is that you will be most engaging if people feel valued in their relationship with you. Put it another way, if people feel listened to by you, feel that their opinion matters to you, believe that you actively want them involved, and get acknowledged by you, then you'll be going a long way to engaging them. At best, your relationship with them gives them a feeling of being in partnership with you, up to something together.

To get the power of this aspect, go to the flip-side for a moment. How engaged would you be by someone whom you felt didn't value your opinion, didn't listen to you, you didn't feel acknowledged by, and you got no sense of partnership from? Almost certainly you'd not be engaged.

And you can check this for yourself with these prompts:

- Describe the nature and feel of the relationship you have with people you are readily engaged by.

- Now describe it with people you're not engaged by.

- Similarly, what do you see about your relationships with people you easily engage and those you don't?

Be in no doubt – engaging others is so much easier when it's underpinned by a Big Relationship. And this happens when people see that you are real and authentic. They feel they can trust you and be safe around you and this has them believe in you and what it is that you want. Your challenge then is clear – to build these bigger relationships with all the people who you want to lead.

> "Now we have to add another denomination: we must develop the ability to form relationships in such a way that people get a whole lot more done a whole lot quicker. Trusting, supportive, and energising relationships are the new currency."
>
> John Childress

2 Possibilities, Ideas

You will help yourself engage others if you create a sense of possibilities about the Future, and ideas of how things could be. This is how you can lift the spirits of people, spark their Spirit Energy, raise their optimism and sense of hope.

But again, notice how your focus is different in Engage from what it was in Future.

In Future, your job is to connect with Possibilities that lift your spirits. However, in Engage the key is to spark Possibilities in others that are meaningful to them.

This is a shift of focus many leaders don't figure out. They can be excited about the Future and can automatically assume others will be too. Sometimes others might be. But what you've really got to do is help people see Possibilities for themselves and what they care about in what's being explored.

Put it another way, where does engagement take place? It takes place over there in other people, so your job is to help ignite Possibilities over there – and not be content just because you're pretty excited over here.

So how can you share what you're up to in a way that sparks Possibilities in others? My one-word answer is **Co-invention**. This can be the most powerful way of helping people move up the Levels of Engagement – by inviting them in to co-invent Possibilities of

- what the Future could be like,
- what 'great' would look like,
- what we'd need to work on to get there,
- what could be some next steps,
- how we would need to work together, and so on.

In other words, you will engage people more by valuing them and asking them to be involved in the thinking about the Future rather than you simply delivering a finished vision. This doesn't mean you ignore what it is you care about. Rather, it means also inviting Co-invention that builds others' sense of ownership for what you are leading for. Some of the art of leading is bringing your leadership for what you care about and inviting Co-invention at the same time. As ever, you'll improve with Conscious Practice.

> "If I were to wish for anything I should not wish for wealth and power, but for the passionate sense of what can be, for the eye which sees the possible. Pleasure disappoints, possibility never. And what wine is so sparkling, so intoxicating as possibility?"
>
> Søren Kierkegaard

3 Opportunities, Priorities

After watching many leaders engage their colleagues, I've concluded that getting things right in the bottom two boxes of the Pyramid – Relationships and Possibilities – is where engagement stands or falls.

However, working here alone leaves room for people to go off in all sorts of directions – and this may not be appropriate if you want them to focus in on particular Opportunities and Priorities.

It's also worth saying that some people connect more quickly to more tangible ideas than to what can seem intangible Possibilities. Sometimes you can help people get to the 'oh, I see' moment by being more specific about what you want to work on together.

For example, you may want to link the idea of being 'the best company or team in the field' with the Priorities of being specifically the best at service, quality, rate of innovation or focus on customer, client or patient in order to engage the full energy of people. That is, this is where some serious planning is done, to convert broad ideas into specific areas you'll choose to focus on.

Again, you can raise the Level of Engagement by inviting Co-invention here. For example, you may want others' views on what areas of Opportunity they believe you should focus on if you're to be the best. Or if you have decided on the Opportunities you'll focus on, you might ask, 'How do you see we can excel in the areas we are going to focus on or how would we need to work differently to excel in these areas?' Such Co-invention builds ownership and prepares for action.

4 Actions

Leadership doesn't end with engaging people. It ends with Deliver – that is, Possibilities getting focused into specific Opportunities, and then Results being delivered through focused Actions.

On the bridge from Engage to Deliver are the conversations you have about what Actions are needed. At the core of these conversations are Requests and Promises. If you want to move yourself and others into Action mode, move from co-inventing ideas and sharing opinions and points of view into making powerful Requests and Promises. Let me explain.

Just as I believe that

Leaders build Big Relationships

I also say that

Leaders make Big Requests.

Many of us hold back here – yes, it's those Limiting Beliefs again that can get in the way. But in your best Leader Mode, you ask for what you want. You're Guided by the Future you Want and you make Big Requests in line with it. Standing by your Promises and helping others do the same with the help of your Requests ensures that you turn ideas and dreams about the Future into reality. So just consider for a moment:

- How well developed is your Leadership Muscle of making Big Requests?

- To what extent in life are you strong in asking for what you want?

- In which situations and relationships do you ask fully for what you want?

- What's holding you back when you don't make the Request you'd really like to?

The good news here is that whatever you're like at the moment you can become much more effective as a leader through the Conscious Practice of making Big Requests.

And one way to practise, both ahead of and during conversations, is to ask yourself the question, 'If I could have anything at all here, what would it be?' Then practise making the Request.

> "The capacity to establish high performance-improvement expectations continues to be the most universally underdeveloped skill."
>
> Robert Schaffer

To summarise then

The wonderful Pyramid model lays out in a simple way the four spaces that need to be addressed for people to work together to deliver excellent results. It also shows you the four aspects of Engage that you'll need to attend to.

They are:

1 Your engaging of others happens inside your Relationships and engagement happens a lot faster inside Big Relationships.

2 Engagement is fuelled by Possibilities that others can see for themselves linked to the Future they want. Co-invention can be immensely powerful at sparking these Possibilities and raising the Level of Engagement.

3 Engagement is then sharpened by agreement on the specific Opportunities and Priorities to be focused on.

4 And the bridge to Deliver is made by making Big Requests of others to elicit Promises to take Action.

You can grow rapidly as an engaging leader through your Conscious Practice. To maximise your rate of growth I want to finish this chapter by pointing you towards three muscle-building practices.

Three 'Engage' Practices

1 Consciously Practise 'Engaging' rather than 'Transmitting/Communicating'

Your interactions with others will be a mix of 'transmitting, telling, presenting and reporting' to them and 'engaging' them. But how many of those instances could be opportunities you take to engage people in you and what you are up to? The answer is certainly more than you've been aware of to date.

When you're up to something, you're actively looking for opportunities to engage people. So do this consciously. Make it a Conscious Practice and, of course, get feedback from others about when you're engaging and when you're not. Find out what it is about you that helps you be engaging and how you sometimes work against yourself. You cannot know how you come across to others. Get feedback.

2 Consciously Practise Building Big Relationships

You can tell by now how crucial I believe your Relationships are to being an effective leader. I've learnt to emphasise this point because it's not at all obvious to many leaders who believe that it's their thinking and their ability to be persuasive in argument that wins people's commitment.

But don't be the Operator/Manager who is focused solely on getting the task done.

In Leader Mode, you don't just get the job done, you also consciously build the Relationship at the same time.

Think about it. In each of your interactions, you're either building your Relationship or you're not. Why not practise getting the job done and building the Relationship too? That way, the current task will likely be done better and faster and you create the ground for more to be done together in the future.

Your influence and impact as a leader arrives via your Relationships. Consciously build them big enough to get the job done. This will require you being really effective at the third practice.

> "Increasingly, the best of breed lead not by virtue of power alone, but by excelling in the art of relationship, the singular expertise that the changing business climate renders indispensable."
>
> Goleman, Boyatzis and McKee

3 Consciously Manage your 'Shadow of a Leader'

Can you think of someone who, when they walk into your work area, immediately dampens your spirits and flattens your energy? Can you also think of someone who, when they come over, whatever you're doing, has the reverse impact and lifts your spirits and has you feel more lively?

This is such a fascinating phenomenon. People arrive in your space and, before a word is spoken, you can feel different. I describe this by saying that each of us at different times shines our **Light** and casts the **Shadow of a Leader**.

By answering the questions above, I'm sure you could quickly identify the Shadow some people cast on you, and the Light that some bring. But here are some big questions for you about you as an engaging leader:

- How well do you know what the Light is that you bring and the Shadow you cast?
- How well do you know how your Light and Shadow impact different people?
- How well do you know which of your Relationships are limited because you are casting a Shadow on another but are not aware of it?

The fact is that, by yourself, you cannot work out the answers to these questions. Again, this is where you need your Support Team. And here's a way into the conversation with them. Get clear on the impact you want to have on people around you, your Impact Intended. But then realise that this counts for nothing compared with your Impact Felt – the impact you actually have on people as experienced by them.

I guarantee there will be times when not only will you not be having the impact you intend but you won't have been aware of it.

I'll always remember working with a very capable leader, Sandy, and his team. Sandy was very sharp and wanted an Impact Intended that had colleagues feeling listened to and valued while stretched and challenged. However, when I asked his peers and reports to describe how they felt around Sandy it included 'steam-rollered, trampled on, not good enough, and left thinking "why did I bother?"'

This was absolutely not Sandy's Impact Intended and he was shocked to learn that at times this was his Impact Felt.

Of course, it was only by learning about his Shadow that Sandy could do anything about it – and it's the same for you. To grow fast, learn about your Light and your Shadow. Ask colleagues how you impact their energy, how they feel, what they see is possible and what is not when they are with you. I've also found this sort of feedback on the home front pretty enlightening too!!

With this learning, you can then become a lot smarter at managing the impact of your Shadow wherever you are. In turn, this will help you build bigger Relationships and engage people even more to respond positively to your Big Requests to build the Future you want.

> "The culture of a company is the behaviour of its leaders. Leaders get the behaviour they exhibit and tolerate. You change the culture of a company by changing the behaviour of its leaders. You measure the change in culture by measuring the change in the personal behaviour of its leaders and the performance of the business."
>
> Dick Brown

In summary …

When you're a leader up to something, every interaction is an opportunity to engage others in you and the Future. Why not practise being your engaging best in many more of these situations? Build those Relationships, bring your Light and manage that Shadow.

FED IN PRACTICE

LUCY KIDD

Lucy Kidd was a client of ours at Unilever and is now one of the Steve Radcliffe Associates team. She has an interesting take on the importance of engagement.

'Something I'm practising at the moment is to notice when I'm resisting something and then to choose instead to fully engage with it – to go with the flow and see where it takes me.

'I was working on a document when my four-year old son called for me. I could immediately feel myself resisting his interruption, but chose in

▶

the moment to let this go. Instead, I took a deep breath and decided to fully engage with him.

'He wanted to show me the "fox den" that he had just built under the bedcovers. My "resisting self" would have tucked him in, said "good night" and hurried back to my computer! Instead, I crawled in with him and became a "fox mummy" for a while! I came back to my writing with a smile on my face and warmth in my heart. By choosing to engage rather than resist I had not only connected more positively with my son but had also been energised by it.

'When we choose to fully engage, we give ourselves totally. Through letting go of our resistance and choosing instead to engage, we can connect with what is really important to us. It isn't easy but when we do we may find it fuels our energy and helps us bring our best.

'So notice what you resist. Notice how this resistance affects your energy and how it would be to engage. These questions might help you:

- What is the source of your resistance?

- How could you let go of this? (e.g. deep breath or connect to the bigger picture.)

- What else could you do to fully engage?'

Future–Engage–**Deliver**

... the focus is not on how well you deliver, it's how well you deliver through others.

- Future–Engage–**Deliver**
- Deliver *through Others*
- Deliver More Now
    - **1** To excel in Deliver, you must first have done a great job in Future and Engage
    - **2** To excel in Deliver, you have to mean it!
- Deliver More Later
- Putting it all into Practice
- The Leader's Conversations for Delivery

Future–Engage–Deliver

You can see it every day in the papers – instances of organisations not delivering; not delivering aspirations, strategies, plans, levels of quality and service, goals, results. That must mean there are an awful lot of leaders out there not delivering!

At the same time, I know that this needn't be the case. I have learnt so much from sitting alongside leaders who have delivered through the people around them.

In this chapter, I will point you towards ideas and practices that can significantly increase your capacity to Deliver in two regards. First, there are practices to take on in order for you to Deliver More Now. Second, there are practices that help you build the capacity to deliver in those around you, and thereby Deliver More Later.

But first I want to ensure you're thinking about Deliver from your Leader Mode and not as Operator/Manager. Let me tell you about Larry.

Deliver *through Others*

Larry was the Head of Manufacturing at the Los Angeles cosmetics company I used to run. He knew every nut and bolt in the place having been there for decades. As a marketeer by training, I knew very little about these places called 'factories'! So I asked my friend and manufacturing expert, Mike, to come over and tell me what he saw.

Mike thought the place was well run but he made one memorable comment. He told me that, while Larry should continue to make sure that all the lines ran well, from now on he should never physically touch a machine again!

What Mike had identified was that Larry was an excellent Operator/Manager who, through his expertise, was delivering well. But if we were to succeed in our ambition to expand the business across the USA, he would need to grow into a leader who Delivered *through Others.*

We all know how to get something done, to Deliver. Your ability to deliver is one of the qualities that helps move your career forward. And sometimes you will have to deliver in your Operator/Manager Mode. But beware, this strength can be your weakness, particularly when people need you in Leader Mode.

It's easy at times to fall back to, 'Oh, it's quicker if I do it myself'. Or you might get a kick out of saying, 'Yea, give that to me, I'll show you how to do it'. But this is a mistake if you are trying to Deliver *through Others.*

The first step then in being brilliant at delivery as a leader is to make sure you are in the right mode.

In Leader Mode, your first thought is not 'what shall I do?' It's 'who do I want to Engage and what is the Request I want to make of them?'

This is a shift in mindset and one that some budding leaders don't make. In Chapter 4, I introduced the idea that 'Leaders make Big Requests'. Yes, we are here again. This is an essential Leadership Muscle. We all have it but I've found that most of us can grow this muscle substantially.

Pause for a while and notice what you're like:

● How strong is your tendency just to do a job yourself?

● Is making requests of others your first or second thought?

● Who are the people you do make requests of?

● Who are the people you don't?

● How clear is your picture of you delivering in Leader Mode rather than in Operator/Manager Mode?

So take on the Conscious Practice of first noticing whether your inclination is to do a job yourself, then choosing not to. Instead, practise making Big Requests of others. I'll help you get even clearer on these Deliver practices later but, for now, I want to make sure you're clear about the next two factors you have to be excellent at to consistently Deliver More Now.

> "No company can deliver on its commitments or adapt well to change unless all leaders practise the discipline of execution at all levels. Execution has to be a part of a company's strategy and its goals. It is the missing link between aspirations and results."
>
> Larry Bossidy

Deliver More Now

My learnings from meeting Derek point to two essential factors in the territory of Deliver.

Derek was the chief executive of a billion-pound-plus business. With his team, he had developed goals for the business, a clearly articulated strategy, detailed plans by brand and customer, clarity of what would be measured and good financial controls. This data was translated into department and individual targets and progress was monitored regularly. All very thorough.

And yet, despite all this, the business did not deliver!

It missed its targets, slid into decline and Derek was moved on. As a leader, Derek had not brought the two ingredients I have seen as essential if you want high levels of delivery through others.

1 To excel in Deliver, you must first have done a great job in Future and Engage.

Deliver is not a standalone aspect of leading. It follows directly on from Future and Engage. This is captured in the story of the two stone-carvers. You meet the first one and ask him what he's doing and he replies, 'I'm carving stone'. You then ask the second, more motivated carver and he says, 'I'm building a cathedral'.

What the story tells us is that when you need people to deliver consistently for you, you cannot ask them simply to carve more stone and then some more! You have to help them imagine a powerful sense of a bigger, more compelling Future. And you'll need to Engage them in that Future so that they are feeling it's not 'your cathedral', it's 'our cathedral'. Derek had done neither.

To get your own perspective on this point, answer these questions now:

- How well do you Deliver when you feel you're just being asked to carve more stone?

- How differently do you behave when you feel you're part of building a cathedral?

- What extra human energies, qualities and drives do you bring when you're building cathedrals?

So excellence in Deliver first requires excellence in Future and Engage. If you're not seeing the levels of delivery you want from others, first think through what sort of job you've done in Future and Engage.

Even more importantly, check with them to find out what sort of job they say you've done.

> "Vision without Action is merely a dream. Action without Vision is merely passing time. Vision with Action can change the world."
>
> Nelson Mandela

2 To excel in Deliver, you have to mean it!

Even when you're alive with a Future you want and you've engaged people, there will still be forces working against you delivering brilliantly through others. In order to counter these forces, you need to bring yourself in a certain way to the Deliver aspect of leading.

While people may want to deliver with you, they are also human. They become distracted; they lose the plot; they make mistakes; they forget; they get different messages from different departments; they become unclear about what they're trying to do and why; they become disheartened because they don't believe they have the tools for the job or they see others working against them. You can probably add to the list when you think about what limits delivery in your organisation.

Leaders who deliver recognise that these factors exist and they bring their own vital energies to counterbalance these forces. Other writers make this point. Jim Collins' research found that the leaders best at delivering brought *Fierce Resolve* and Larry Bossidy et al. identified that having *Emotional Fortitude* is vital for high levels of execution. Others write about the need for *Focus*, *Discipline* and *Resilience*.

You already have these human qualities. They are a part of how you are at certain times in your life. But how do you effortlessly bring them to the Deliver aspect of leading? My answer is by having what you want delivered be a part of what you are leading for, which in turn is deeply connected to what you care about. In other words the focus of Deliver is an important piece of the Future you want.

This is a crucial connection but one that is easy to lose. Yes, it makes sense to translate your aspirations for the Future you want into targets and results that you can focus on now.

But many organisations in private and public sectors make these measures the end in themselves while losing sight of the overall ambition.

So keep on asking yourself big picture questions like, 'What's our overall purpose here?', 'What does glorious success look like?' and 'To have the Future we want, what other factors should we pay attention to as well as those we measure?'

When what you want to be delivered matters to you, you can lead powerfully in Deliver. You will have high expectations and set high standards. You will keep a focus when others may be distracted, follow through and follow up and you will hold people to account. And you and others will naturally put in place those practical aspects of delivery – plans, milestones, processes and timetables – to ensure timely delivery.

Crucially, you will more likely be strong in an area I see lots of leaders holding back from – the handling of poor performance. A pattern I see often is a leader doing so much to have people deliver but then undoing much of this good work by not facing up to poor performance. Yes, I know conversations here can be uncomfortable, but you can push through that discomfort if what you want is part of what's important to you and what you care about. The more you mean it, the more you will not tolerate poor performance.

And when people see that you mean it, it impacts their behaviour. To take a simple example, one of my sons, Alex, like many teenagers, used to be extremely untidy. From an early age, when his Mum asked him to tidy his room, he'd immediately assess, 'Does she mean it or not?' Depending on his reading of Mum, he'd then get into action or not.

Similarly, a friend said to me the other day, 'We used to really perform when we worked for Terry; you could just tell he expected us to deliver, so we did.'

What's happening in both these situations is captured in the line:

Forgive me. I cannot hear what you're saying because who you are being is shouting at me!

In other words, in many of our interactions, people are reading 'who we are being' behind our words. And in the realm of Deliver this is crucial.

People around you are constantly reading:

- Is what you're asking of others important to you?
- Do you mean it?
- Are you bringing urgency and conviction or anxiety or hesitation to your requests?
- Are you likely to follow up on what you're asking for?

I've come to realise by watching the most effective leaders that it is these aspects of authenticity that take delivery to whole new levels. The best plans and timetables won't on their own suffice. You must bring powerful aspects of your being to bear if you want to bring the best out of others. To take you back to Derek, he hadn't engaged his people in a compelling Future and they didn't get that he meant it. Consequently they didn't deliver.

I will soon introduce a model that will help you be conscious of what you're like in these Deliver aspects of leading so that you can Deliver More Now.

"Cain didn't have the kind of inspiring personality that would galvanise the company. But he had something much more powerful; inspired standards. He could not stand mediocrity in any form. For the next 14 years, he relentlessly imposed his will for greatness on Abbott Labs."

Jim Collins

IN PRACTICE

ROB WILSON

Professor Robert Wilson is Medical Director and Surgeon at South Tees Acute NHS Foundation Trust and Professor of Surgical Science at the University of Durham. He's very grateful to have had a colleague introduce him to FED. He writes:

'I start a new job next month as Medical Director of the healthcare trust where I have been working as a consultant surgeon for well over 20 years. This has been the single most significant thing in my recent professional life. It has re-energised me and, thanks to the help of my colleague, Peter Lees, who is a great believer in FED, I too have become an enthusiast.

'I'm certainly going to need all the help I can get. As the most senior doctor in an organisation of near enough 1,000 medical staff and more than 7,000 staff in total, I will be responsible for leading my part in strategy and governance over the next five years or so.

'But what of the really big leadership challenges that interested me in the job in the first place? For me to be really up to something and deal with these new challenges will require energetic application of all the principles of FED.

'Already I am stretching some of the FED leadership muscles. I have a clear vision of the future, I'm past the starting gate and on my way. With this positive energy I know that I am engaging others in this future and see the challenge of the financial context that we face as a great opportunity for us all. I really know that so long as I keep practising stretching these Future and Engage muscles that we will Deliver – together! And finally I know that, as a leader who is up to something big, I need to keep growing my support team – and I thank my senior colleagues for coaching me on this exciting leadership journey.'

Deliver More Later

Much of what's needed to Deliver More Now is about getting the best from yourself and others today. Much of Deliver More Later is about growing yourself and others so that the capability to Deliver increases into the future. That is, the best today gets even better in the future.

Encouragingly, I see more and more leaders committing to developing their people. Often, however, I see their approach limited by their dated thinking about leadership. The result is that I see many leaders developing people as *good, quality followers*. However, if you want to excel at delivering more later, my encouragement to you is to Develop Others *as Leaders*, and this is quite different.

A lot of the old thinking about leadership was based on the idea of one leader and lots of followers. However, this thinking limits both people's growth and the levels of delivery possible. Author John Kotter rails against this thinking when he writes:

> *'The notion of having one or two leaders in a large organisation is ridiculous. The trouble is that people have convinced themselves that leadership isn't their job. My vision is to create 100 million new leaders. That's not 100 million CEOs. But it is a question of enabling many, many more people to provide leadership in their jobs, no matter what their jobs are.'*

This echoes where I'm coming from. We are all leaders. It's not a position that comes from our title or age. As we explored early on, people around you have a number of ways of limiting themselves as leaders and you can make a material difference to their growth as leaders. You can do this by helping them distinguish their Leader Mode from the Operator/Manager one they will know well, by helping them see how they can grow their Leadership Muscles, and even by helping them identify and go beyond their Limiting Beliefs.

I encourage you to take everything you are learning here and elsewhere and bring it to the job of Developing Others as Leaders. Your impact by doing this can be enormous. Indeed one writer, Noel Tichy, concludes after 25 years of consulting:

> 'winning companies win because they have good leaders who nurture the development of other leaders at all levels of the organisation'.

So pause for a while and think about what being great at Developing Others as Leaders might look like for you. How would you need to think? How would you approach conversations with them? When would you ask questions rather than give answers? What would you need to know from them about how they want to be and grow?

Here are some prompts for you that will help make you strong in this area:

- You commit to Developing Others as Leaders because it's a core ingredient in your beliefs about how you're going to succeed. If you do it because someone told you to or it's the latest HR initiative, you won't be great at it.

- You develop a mindset that doesn't just focus on getting the job done now but also constantly looks for opportunities to grow others. We can all get so sucked into the immediacy of delivering now that we lose sight of investing in the future.

- You encourage them to explore the topics in Chapter 3. That is, you encourage them to think about 'what they care about', 'what they want to lead for' and 'who they want to be as a leader'. Yes, you'll have some views you'll offer on how you see them and how you'd like them to grow but you add these to their thinking about who is the leader they want to be.

- You'll demonstrate that you too are practising growing yourself as a leader, rather than just expecting others to do it. At its very best, you help each other to grow so that you are an integral part of each other's Support Team.

The old leadership game was hierarchical and mostly one-way. The new game is one in which everyone helps grow each other. In some organisations, I've helped create what I call a Community of Leaders in which everyone knows they are working at growing themselves as leaders and everyone joins in to help grow each other. Results have included spectacular growth of people and levels of delivery.

How does where you and your organisation are now compare with what's possible?

● How much is Developing Others as Leaders a strong part of the culture?

● Who do you have developing you as a leader?

● Who would you like to have? and

● What can you do to arrange this?

● Who are you developing as leaders?

● Who could you be? and

● What difference could that make to what's Delivered Now and Later?

> "The function of leadership is to produce more leaders, not more followers."
>
> Ralph Nader

Putting it all into Practice

Briefly then, if you want to Deliver then you have to be thinking and acting from your Leader Mode. That way, you'll be looking to Deliver *through Others*. You must also ensure you've first done a great job at the Future and Engage aspects of leading. And to really Deliver More Now, you have to mean it. To ensure you Deliver More Later, don't just look to develop those around you, develop them as leaders. It's a mindset and requires Conscious Practice.

So how do you put all this into practice? The answer lies in what you're like in The Leader's Conversations for Delivery.

The Leader's Conversations for Delivery

As ever, I want to help you be a more Conscious Leader. In the Future aspect of leading, I've encouraged you to be conscious of who you are being – are you being an Operator/Manager or Leader in touch with what you care about? In Engage, I've steered you towards being conscious of your relationships – are they big enough to get the job done? Now in Deliver, I want to help you heighten your awareness of what you're like in your conversations – are they a Leader's Conversations for Delivery?

It is through your conversations with people that you stimulate Delivery *through Others*. It's here that you show up as a leader, engaging and meaning it – or not. It's been fascinating over the years noticing the quality of conversation in different organisations. In the most successful, the nature of conversation is what I and others call **Robust Dialogue**. That is, adult to adult, straightforward, grown-up conversation that gets to the truth of the matter. Different points of view are listened to and, when decisions are made, they are committed to. In too many other organisations, the space to challenge and speak the truth doesn't seem to be there. Yes, decisions are made but they are gone along with rather than committed to. Check in now. How well would you say your organisation does Robust Dialogue? How well do you?

Though delivery can seem immensely complex, I've realised that it's really about just four conversations. Make these more robust and I guarantee you will deliver more. I'll first outline the four conversations and how they hang together. Then we'll take each in turn to help you identify where you want to be stronger. This is how they look in time:

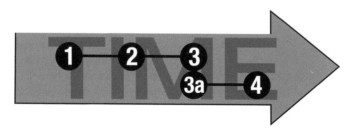

Conversation 1. Making Big Requests: this is where you make the request for delivery. Ideally it is made in a way that has others engaged by the Future you want and leaves them wanting to deliver what's needed.

Conversation 2. Maximising Probability of Delivery: this is the ongoing conversation you have until the result is achieved. Its purpose is to maximise the probability of delivery.

Conversation 3. Delivery is Acknowledged: this is the conversation you have when what you want is delivered at the time and to the standard you'd like. Here is a major opportunity to build more capability to Deliver More Later.

Conversation 3a. Non-delivery is Addressed: this is the conversation you have when what you wanted has not been delivered or to the standard you'd like. It can require some Emotional Fortitude from you but it also provides another great opportunity to build more capability to Deliver More Later.

Conversation 4. The Wrap-up: here is the wrap-up conversation when the job is eventually completed.

Having explored these conversations with thousands of people, there is a promise I can make to you. It's that you will not yet be brilliant at all these conversations and, as you look at each one in turn, you will definitely find ways you can be stronger at one or more of them.

Another reason I'm confident with my promise is that in our interactions with others there are always things we'd prefer to avoid. It'll be different for each of us but we may want to avoid being seen as too aggressive or demanding; we may want to avoid the risk of setting back our relationships; we may want to avoid being rejected or not liked. We'll all have our favourites linked to our personal Limiting Beliefs! You may want to think about what holds you back at times with each conversation.

With that perspective, let's look at each conversation. I'll provide a checklist for the main ingredients you might want in the conversation. I suggest you read them through now to identify where you are already naturally strong and which ingredients you will consciously practise bringing to your Deliver interactions with others.

You can also then come back to the list before or after crucial Deliver conversations to help your Conscious Practice. To help you do this, you can print off this next section at **www.futureengagedeliver.com/book**.

Before you dive in, just get in touch with how you are when you are at your very best in this area. Think of a time when there was something really important to you that you wanted others to Deliver for you, i.e. you really meant it. Get in touch with the energies you brought to your conversations. Notice how robust you were. With that perspective in your mind, reflect on how you can be in these conversations:

Conversation 1
Making Big Requests

● Are you clear on what you want, by when and to what standard? If not, are you ready to invite others in, in order to get this clear?

● At the end of the conversation, you may be clear but how will you know if others are? (I used to be great at being crystal clear on what I wanted but it never crossed my mind to check whether others were!)

● Are you looking to engage others or just 'communicate at' them? Or at times do you ask them to 'just carve more stone'?

● Similarly, are you seeing this as a one-way conversation or a two-way dialogue and Co-invention that helps build others' involvement and ownership?

● If you are looking to engage them, is the Relationship big enough to get the job done, or will you need to build it further as a part of this conversation?

● Are you focused only on Possibilities that excite you? Or are you sparking Possibilities for others so they feel that the 'cathedral' is theirs too?

- Can the Request you're making be delivered within the current ways of working/the current culture? Or are you also asking for new ways of thinking and behaviours? In Leader Mode, at times you will want to and need to make these bigger Requests.

- What human aspects of delivery are needed and are you bringing them? Are you bringing conviction, urgency, passion, enthusiasm, belief that you can do it together?

- Finally, are you also designing Conversation 2, i.e. how are you going to work together to ensure you all do a great job here?

Of course, you don't need every ingredient present each time you make a request – you may not need to be passionate when you ask, 'Can you pass me a copy of the agenda?' The key is to be conscious and bring what's needed in each instance.

Conversation 2
Maximising Probability of Delivery

- Echoing the above, are you talking up front on how you'll work together to ensure delivery?

- Are you agreed on how you'll be kept up to date on progress? In what form and how frequently?

- Are you agreed on what you want to know and when after setbacks or missed milestones?

- And are you creating a safe space so that people feel safe to tell you of setbacks and bad news?

▶

- Are you ready to offer appropriate input, support and coaching to help keep others focused and delivering?

- At the same time, are you also bringing a commitment and resolve that others see and respond to?

- Overall, are you helping others manage their energy towards successful delivery?

I'll always remember a very capable leader announcing 'I've just realised, I don't do this Conversation!' And that may be ok with some people some of the time. As a Conscious Leader, however, it's up to you to choose what's needed in each instance.

Conversation 3
Delivery is Acknowledged

I can't emphasise enough how powerful this Conversation 3 can be at helping people grow and so Deliver More Later. A number of these conversations over time can massively build people's confidence, self-belief and thereby capacity to deliver more. I'm putting so much weight behind this point because I've seen many instances of the power of this confidence-building – but I've met few leaders who are naturally strong in this conversation. It's as if we just don't recognise the power we have to help others feel good about themselves and what they can achieve.

Pause for a second and remember a time when you felt brilliant after someone had acknowledged you for what you'd done or how you'd gone about it. Please take on board as fully as you can that you have the same power to have people around you feeling similarly good about themselves. So …

- Are you free in acknowledging others for a good job done? Or are you closer to the school of, 'No, I don't acknowledge a good job done. That's what they get paid for'?

- Potentially more important, are you free in acknowledging the person for what they have contributed to progress? 'Really good job, thanks,' from you will help someone feel valued. However, acknowledgement of the person, not just the job done, like, 'I want you to know I really appreciate the creativity you brought to this challenge, the way you kept everyone focused, and the tenacity you showed to get it all done on time. Many thanks,' can help someone's confidence grow even more. Whatever you do, don't try to fake being sincere in your feedback. Either mean it or keep quiet!

- With those you are developing as leaders, do you ask what they have learned about themselves and who they could be as a leader?

- Do you pause to extract the learning from this success rather than just bashing on with the next challenge?

- Also, do you pause to consider what's possible now that didn't seem possible earlier?

- Overall, do you leave others feeling good about themselves, wanting to grow even further and ready to take on even more?

Conversation 3a
Non-delivery is Addressed

Here, quality delivery on time is not achieved. This is the conversation many people prefer to avoid or at least dilute. But if you're in touch with

▶

what you care about and really want delivered, you'll be less inclined to fudge this conversation.

What can also help is if you speak to others with the mindset of wanting them to succeed and grow. If you want someone to grow and you see them performing poorly in some way, do you keep quiet? Not if you care about them and their progress. Certainly not if you are committed to helping them develop as a leader. So …

- Are you having this conversation as soon as you can or are you putting it off? At worst, with someone who works for you, are you keeping quiet and storing it up till the annual appraisal?

- Are you speaking your truth about what you see and how you feel about it while also listening to their view?

- Are you maximising the learning from the situation?

- Are you making clear the consequences of repeated under-delivery? I can take you to quite a few organisations that could achieve so much more if the leaders were stronger at making just this one aspect of Deliver clearer.

- Are you agreeing a new timeline for delivery?

- Are you bringing commitment and determination to getting the job done? Are you bringing truthfulness and openness helped by wanting others to learn and grow?

- Overall, are you having this conversation in a way that lifts the other's energy – either immediately or soon after – rather than lowering their energy and confidence?

Conversation 4
The Wrap-up

Here delivery finally happens and in many respects this conversation is similar to Conversation 3 in the acknowledgement of a job done. But there is a powerful piece to add here because this is the conversation where you as a leader can help your colleague recognise something vital about themself. We all sometimes trip up or meet unexpected obstacles and how we engage with difficulties is part of our leadership journey. There may be deeper learning about ourselves available at these times. Consider exploring this deeper territory with your colleague – it will certainly help you both develop faster as leaders:

- What beliefs did your colleague have about themself when they didn't get it right first time?

- What might they have been tempted to do, e.g. avoid, hide, not take responsibility?

- What support did they look for and get in tackling the difficulty faced? Did they turn to their Support Team?

- What qualities did they need to bring to rectify the situation?

- What did they learn from the experience?

- And how have they grown?

"In order to get a real conversation, you have to drop artificial language, you have to drop politics and you have to drop an environment based on fear and hiding. People must be encouraged not only to know their craft, products, their work, but to know a little of themselves."

David Whyte

In summary ...

Reflect back on what you are like as a leader who delivers:

- What have you noticed about yourself and your Leader's Conversations for Delivery?

- Where are you naturally strong and not so strong?

- Could you be even stronger at delivering by making more explicit the connection with what you care about and what you are leading for?

- Crucially, how do your colleagues see you in these Conversations?

- How could you get more feedback on this aspect of your leadership?

- Which ingredients of which Conversations will you take on as part of your Conscious Practice?

- Who in your Support Team will you ask to give you regular feedback on what you're going to practise?

FED IN PRACTICE

JASON DANIELS

Jason Daniels is a Safety, Health and Environment Manager who wrote to us about his breakthrough moment in developing his colleagues.

'How often in my role as an emerging business leader do I find myself eagerly offering people the answers to the problems they are grappling with? I know at such moments that I'm busy on the hamster wheel and only later do I remember that there might have been a more effective way to engage colleagues in what they were delivering.

'Then after a recent FED coaching session, I took stock and considered again how my Shadow as a leader might be impacting on others. I recognised that if I was going to really develop my team of people as leaders then I would have to change my approach. So I made the decision to make time to consciously practise holding back from using my intellectual energy and giving easy answers, and instead encourage people to show their invention and express their creativity.

'So in the next team project meeting, I purposefully asked inviting questions and held them long enough for people to emerge with more purposeful enquiries of their own.

'The result was transformational. Instead of it being about my solutions, they discovered their answers. As a consequence, they have chosen to lead for change with this project, chosen to engage with key stakeholders within the business and have started to envisage many future benefits that the end product of this project can be used for.

'The reward for me? Fulfilment! Fulfilment in seeing them excited and energised about the project ahead, of seeing them continue with further ideas of their own, and of their vision of just what is possible and of what the end goal will be. I'm now asking a lot more questions and seeing people perform in ways I hadn't thought was possible.'

The Four Energies

... don't just use your intellect, engage people's emotions and spirit too.

- The Four Energies
- The story of Adrian ... and the thousands like him!!
- The Four Energies
  - Intellectual Energy
  - Emotional Energy
  - Spirit Energy
  - Physical Energy
- The Energies in Your Organisation
- The Energies and You
- 'Future' and The Energies
- 'Engage' and The Energies
  - Relationships: Key Energy, Emotional
  - Possibilities, Ideas: Key Energy, Spirit
  - Opportunities, Priorities: Key Energy, Intellectual
  - Actions: Key Energy, Physical
- 'Deliver' and The Energies
- And finally

The Four Energies

Peter Drucker was the granddaddy writer on the topics of leadership and organisations. So when he began one line with 'Your first and foremost job as a leader is …', I sat up and paid attention.

He went on to point to an idea I have found very powerful in helping people grow as leaders:

> *Your first and foremost job as a leader is to manage your own energy, and help manage the energy of those around you.*

At first glance, this can seem a bit odd; there doesn't seem to be anything in there about the Future, Engaging others, Delivery and Results. But as you'll see in this chapter, Drucker is offering another really valuable view of *Future–Engage–Deliver* that can help you be even more effective as a leader now and grow even faster.

The story of Adrian … and the thousands like him!!

You'll have come across an Adrian or two! This Adrian was the Chief Executive of an organisation of tens of thousands of people. He'd got to the top by being bright and working hard. But now his organisation was in tougher, more complex times and wasn't delivering. He worked and pushed even harder but it wasn't making a difference.

I talked with Adrian about the idea of energies and the narrowness of his current approach. I helped him see that he'd got this far primarily through the strength of his **Intellectual Energy** and the application of his **Physical Energy**. But what was needed now for his organisation to perform to a higher level was to engage his people's **Emotional** and **Spirit Energies**.

Initially, Adrian hadn't a clue what I was on about! However, he soon reaped the value of seeing leadership as one continual job of energy handling and harnessing. So let me introduce the fabulous Four Energies and link them directly to *Future–Engage–Deliver* and my favourite Relationships to Results Pyramid we looked at in the Engage chapter (Chapter 4).

> "Simply put, a leader's job is to energise others. Notice that I don't say it's part of the job; it is their job. There is no 'time off' when a leader isn't responsible for energising others. Every interaction a leader has is either going to positively energise those around them or negatively energise them."
>
> Noel Tichy

The Four Energies

One way of looking at people is as a walking bundle of Four Energies which constantly interact and feed off each other. The Energies are there to be tapped into by ourselves and influenced by others. And with practice, you can learn to notice and manage these Energies in yourself and others, and thereby influence and deliver so much more.

As we walk through them, be thinking about your Energies. Which are strong? Which are you in touch with? They are:

Intellectual Energy

This is the energy of your thinking, your analysis, your logic and rationality. It's used in debate and argument. It drives curiosity, creativity, planning and focus. It's also behind criticism and finding fault. It's needed to help people be organised but too much of it can suppress passion and enthusiasm.

Emotional Energy

This is the energy of human connection and relationships. When it's strong and positive, people feel listened to, valued, cared for, even special. It's the binding energy that comes with belonging to a group and feeling included.

When less than positive, people can feel excluded, frustrated, anxious, upset and angry. This is an essential energy for effective teamwork, partnership, alignment and collaboration.

Spirit Energy

This is the energy of vitality, of being alive, of being in touch with what you care about. It's strongly linked to your passion, the Future and a sense of possibility.

Do this now. Think of a time when you'd say your spirits were good, you were up. What was your sense of possibility of the Future in that moment?

I've asked a couple of thousand people this question and they have answered along the lines of, 'The possibilities are boundless. Anything's possible,' etc.

Now think of a time when you'd say your spirits were down, you were flat. What was your sense of possibility of the Future then? Most people reply, 'Nothing seems possible, it seems hopeless,' etc.

Spirit Energy is a crucial leadership energy because it brings hope and optimism to people, and so has them feel more ready and confident to build the Future.

It's the energy that comes with people knowing the *why* of what they are doing, having a sense of purpose, being inspired and having aspirations.

All the related words like *spirit, inspiration, aspiration* and *dispirited* stem from the Latin word, *spiro*, which means 'to breathe life into'. So when you bring your Spirit Energy, you are breathing life into yourself and others. Similarly, the flip-side is that when Spirit Energy is missing, people can feel bored, apathetic and work can feel meaningless, a chore and just 'carving stone'!

> "I take it as a given that Spirit is the most critical element of any organisation. With Spirit of the appropriate quantity, quality, and direction, almost anything is possible. Leaders have one task that outweighs all others: to care for the Spirit."
>
> Harrison Owen

Physical Energy

This is the energy of action, making things happen, of getting things done. This energy is also a key part of our vitality and helps us be alert and maintain concentration and commitment.

We know this energy well when it's absent. We can feel tired, listless, worn out and stressed, particularly if our Spirit Energy is low and we have lost sight of *why* we are doing something. We can help ourselves have more Physical Energy through being smarter with our diet, taking exercise, ensuring we take time to relax and get a good night's sleep.

So we have so much energy to bring to what we care about in life. But life may not always help us to notice and then manage our energy well, never mind influence the energy of those around us. I want to help you see how you can be more conscious of the Energies and so lead yourself and others more effectively. Let's move now to exploring what you see about the Energies in your organisation and in yourself.

The Energies in Your Organisation

Let's build your awareness. What do you notice about the Energies in your organisation?

- Which of the Energies are most valued?
- Which do you need to bring to get on and get promoted?
- What do you see about the balance of Energies?
- How consciously are the Energies managed?
- Are senior players all like Adrian? Or do they move beyond just the Intellectual and Physical Energies?
- Who are the people who raise others' Energies?
- Who drains them?
- What meetings and situations give people Energy?
- Which drain the Energy?

- To what extent is it ok in meetings to talk about how you're feeling, not just what you're thinking?

- How much is people's Spirit Energy lifted by the purpose and aspirations of your organisation?

- How strong is the Emotional Energy of people feeling valued by the organisation?

This is the sea of energy you are swimming in. It may be exactly as you want it or it may be something you as a leader want to change.

One of the reasons I'm keen to help leaders think about their organisation and challenges from the Energies angle is because there seem to be lots of 'Adrians' about with a narrow view of Energies. When I've asked people to describe the energy sea they swim in in their organisation, by far the most common reply is that there are loads of Intellectual Energies and Physical Energies.

However, at times there can be so much Intellectual Energy that it slows decision making and action taking. And when there is an over-reliance on Physical Energy to get things done and little managing of the Emotional and Spirit Energies the result is that people end up tired, drained or stressed. So what's the overall picture in your organisation? And how could you spark new conversations about the Energies and how you want them?

> "Leaders are the stewards of organisational energy – in companies, organisations and even in families. The skilful management of energy, individually and organisationally, makes possible something that we call Full Engagement."
>
> Loehr and Schwartz

The Energies and You

Now turn your awareness to yourself. What do you notice about you and the Energies?

- What do you notice about your Energies when you think about work?

- How do your Energies rise and fall at work?

- Which Energies do you naturally bring?

- Which Energies are not strong for you?
- And crucially, what would others say about you on these two questions?
- What gives you Energy?
- What drains it?
- Who gives you Energy?
- Who drains it? And when you think of these people, what do you notice about the size of the Relationship with them?
- How do you recharge your Energy?
- How smart are you at doing this?
- In particular, how are you at managing your Physical Energy through your diet, sleep and lifestyle?

Drucker suggests that your first and foremost job is to manage your own energy. Second, it's to help others with theirs. So what can you practise to manage the Energies better?

_____

_____

_____

_____

_____

Everything I've written in this book so far has been to help you manage your and others' energy. Let me be clearer on how leading through *Future–Engage–Deliver* can be looked at as an ongoing job of energy management.

'Future' and The Energies

So what is the central message about the Future aspect of leading? It's 'Keep your Spirit Energy alive'.

You're at your best in Future when you're in touch with what you care about; you can see the big picture, the whole; you have a sense of being 'up to something'; and you're Being Guided by the Future you Want. In other words, you're fuelled by your Spirit Energy and are guided by it.

When your Spirit Energy is up, you're alive with what's possible. It's easier to see the big picture, the whole. You can quickly connect with the 'why' you are doing something.

At its deepest, Spirit Energy is about being connected with your purpose, the meaning you are giving your life – your ultimate big picture!

Spirit Energy also powerfully influences other Energies. When your spirits are good, it's easier to feel good about yourself – that's your Emotional Energy – and also imagine being the leader you want to be. Your Physical Energy will be enhanced too; you'll have more of a buzz and be ready to throw yourself into things.

Spirit and Intellectual Energies can combine to help you be creative, think new ideas, imagine the way ahead. So strategy and planning work can be uplifted by a sense of what could be. But beware. If the Intellectual Energy becomes dominant, it can take you straight into how you limit yourself as a leader. I pointed to three powerful ways of limiting ourselves earlier:

- Thinking from the Present,
- 'I can't see How', and
- Our Limiting Beliefs.

All three can hold us back when our Intellectual Energy dominates our Spirit. That's when we lose sight of the Future and our thinking shifts to the detail and difficulties of the present. We can stop ourselves by not knowing how to do something, rather than trusting that the answers will arrive on the way. And we can begin to focus on our Limiting Beliefs, those thoughts we have about ourselves which tell us we won't have the Future we want.

To grow as a leader, take on the following Conscious Practices:

- **Stay connected to What You Care About.**
- **Embrace the Big Picture, the Whole.**

- **Be Guided by the Future you Want.**
- **Use your Support Team to help you manage this crucial Energy of yours.**

Keep your Spirit Energy alive!

'Engage' and The Energies

Just as Future is very much about the first part of Drucker's quote, 'managing your own energy', so Engage is about the second part, 'helping manage the energy of those around you'. This reveals again why to 'Engage' is so different from 'communicate'. When you are in 'communicate' mode, your focus is mostly on yourself and your message. When you're engaging others, your focus is mostly on how others receive the message and what impact it has on their energies; this is a shift many leaders who 'present' and 'transmit' just don't get.

You can do lots to influence how much energy others bring to what you care about. If they are in Resistance or Apathy to what you are leading for, they'll not be bringing much positive energy. If they are in Grudging or Willing Compliance, they'll bring some.

The question is, how do you help manage the energies of others so they become Enrolled or Committed and want to bring their Four Energies? The answer is laid out nicely in the Relationships to Results Pyramid. Each of the boxes leading to Results corresponds to one of the Energies. Here they are:

To fully Engage others involves managing all Four Energies. Here's how it works by box:

Relationships: Key Energy, Emotional

I've said that engaging happens fastest in Big Relationships. Put another way, it happens fastest when there is strong, positive Emotional Energy present. Engagement is strongly influenced by how people *feel* around you. They will respond quite differently to you and what you're leading for depending on how much they feel included, listened to, acknowledged and safe and feel that you are honest and true. In a nutshell, do they feel connected to you and valued by you?

Crucially, how will you find this out? As we have already explored, you bring Light and you cast a Shadow. You have an Impact Intended and an Impact Felt.

Please do not go around believing your Impact Intended is always the one felt, and that you don't at times cast a Shadow. Use your Support Team to get some feedback. Talk to others about the Four Energies and find out how you impact the Emotional Energies of others.

> "The conclusion of the research is that any decision to lead has to include a commitment to enhance, through practice, our emotional breadth as well as our ability to relate to others' emotions."
>
> Terry Pearce

Possibilities, Ideas: Key Energy, Spirit

You'll have worked out that the key energy here is Spirit. But while Future is about your Spirit Energy, in Engage you are looking to influence the Spirit Energy of others. How can you interact with others so that they see Possibilities for themselves, have aspirations, and feel inspired? Here is where Co-invention is so powerful. By asking others to invent the Future or an aspect of it with you, you are helping them connect with what they care about, their Spirit Energy.

Again, get some feedback on your Impact Felt, your Light and Shadow. Ask people how you impact their Spirit Energy, their sense of optimism and 'can do'.

Opportunities, Priorities: Key Energy, Intellectual

I believe that managing the Spirit and Emotional Energies is the core of Engage. However, you've got to talk sense! That is, your listeners' thinking has to be able to connect with what you want to engage them in. At best, you will engage others' Intellectual Energy with a dash of Spirit so that they are bursting with ideas on how they can make the Future real and what Priorities they could focus on.

Actions: Key Energy, Physical

Finally, you want people inclined to bring their Physical Energy and be ready to take action. You engage this energy by making Requests. It's easy to miss this step; you connect with people to engage their Emotional, Spirit and Intellectual Energies but then you don't ask for action. Be conscious – make the Request to bridge from Engage to Deliver.

Now you have a powerful diagnostic tool for any leadership situation. You can look at the situation through the lens of the Pyramid and the Four Energies. For instance, you can notice whether the Relationships are big enough to get the job done – that is, whether the Emotional Energy needed is present. Or whether there is a strong sense of Possibility – that is, whether there is sufficient Spirit Energy. And so on. And you can practise shifting these Energies in order to engage others even more powerfully and move towards Deliver.

'Deliver' and The Energies

Deliver and the Four Energies are pretty straightforward – to be an effective leader in Deliver, you have to do the 'full Drucker'! You have to manage all your Energies and those of people around you and this is a job for every day. In addition, to Deliver More Later, you have to help others get smarter at managing their own and others' Energies.

As we have seen, Deliver requires more than a good intellectual plan and targets. To deliver effectively, you have first to bring the Energies needed in the Future and Engage aspects of leading. Then you need to consistently find and bring that mix of Energies that shows up as Resolve, Determination,

Persistence and Focus. You have to have the energy for Robust Dialogue. And if these Energies are not present, others will immediately spot it and be less inclined to bring their own Energies.

> "One of the worst aspects of some business studies courses is the assumption that business people are rational fools, devoid of emotion or any sense of responsibility. I have known such people. We should not encourage them."
>
> Charles Handy

And finally

Right from the off, I have encouraged you to take on Conscious Practice as an essential part of growing as a leader. I purposely chose the word 'Conscious' because one of the key things to practise in your leadership is being conscious! Conscious of how you are, who you are being. Conscious of what's happening around you, who others are being and how the energy is.

Energy changes by the moment – there's a setback, there's good news or other priorities come along – and each and every time, the energy changes. Your job as leader is to be conscious of how the Energies are in any moment. That way, you have a chance of shifting the energy in the direction you want and bringing the energy that is missing.

This is not a new idea. Lao Tzu wrote seven thousand years ago:

> *'Consciousness or awareness, then, is the source of your ability. Learn to become increasingly conscious.'*

Remember Adrian from the start of the chapter? Well, this is exactly what he did. Initially, he had no awareness of the Energies and didn't recognise that he focused so intently on just two of them, Intellectual and Physical. In time, he became much more aware of all Four Energies, both in himself and around him. In time, managing the Energies simply became a part of how he led the organisation.

For instance, he shifted the Spirit Energy in the boardroom by getting rid of the long, rectangular table and replacing it with a round one. He changed the Emotional Energy in meetings by banning PowerPoint presentations and encouraging truthful, energising conversation. And together he and I helped others learn about the power of managing the Energies. The result was a lot of transformed leaders and one higher-performing organisation.

> "Leadership is not about making clever decisions and doing bigger deals. It is about helping release the positive energy that exists naturally within people."
>
> Henry Mintzberg

In summary ...

Be increasingly conscious of your and others' energy. At any time during the day, you can ask yourself:

- Is your Spirit Energy up because you're connected to what you care about and you have a sense of possibility?

- What's your read of others' Spirit Energy? How will you lift it if it's flat?

- Do you feel emotionally connected to the work in hand and the people around you?

- Do you sense that others feel included and valued by you, even special? If not, how can you help them feel emotionally connected to you and the work?

- Do you have the Intellectual Energy to think things through?

- Are you stretching the thinking of others to draw on the best of their Intellectual Energy?

- Do you have the Physical Energy ready to take action and make things happen?

- Are you helping others manage their Physical Energy so they avoid becoming tired, stressed or listless?

FIONA STARK

Fiona Stark is Director of Corporate Affairs at Eon and a great advocate of FED and the Four Energies. As part of what she's up to, she invited the company's external legal providers to a meeting about how they could work differently together with her and her team. Typically, they would have started with an outline of the business agenda and then proceeded in their normal intellectual way. But Fiona wanted something much more enlivening – something that liberated the Emotional Energy of partnership and the Spirit Energy of what else might be possible.

'I wanted to engage these lawyers in a radically different relationship,' she explained, 'so instead of starting the meeting in the expected way I asked them instead to relax and imagine what a different future could look like, one in which they would be proud of working with us and as passionate about our customers as we are. I invited them to imagine working with us in ways where they'd be bringing their innovative ideas to the table rather than just pitching to us. And I asked them to imagine a relationship where they would be billing us by value rather than by the hour – because at the end of the day our customers are paying their bills.

'It was a real breakthrough day and one we've since built on. The most forward-thinking had already recognised that the old way of working was limited. They now understand our challenges and are working with us in a much more constructive way. The energy is so different and what's really exciting is that they're seeing the opportunities it opens up for themselves while committing to us in exactly the way we had hoped. Not bad for a bunch of intellectual lawyers!'

Be At Your Best, More of the Time

. . . that's your ultimate goal, simply be at your best, more of the time.

- Be At Your Best, More of the Time
- The overview

Be At Your Best, More of the Time

Harry was a senior manager in an organisation headed towards a merger. The Chief Executive had asked me to do all we could to have his senior managers 'confident and on the front foot' ahead of the merger.

When I first met Harry, you absolutely wouldn't have described him as confident! His energy was really flat. He wasn't engaging anyone and questions were beginning to be asked about whether he was delivering or not.

Two months later he was bursting with energy and fully on the front foot. He'd benefited massively by exploring the big idea I introduce in this chapter. Indeed, he gave me the chapter title. At the end of the leadership programme I'd worked with him on, he said, 'I've figured out what you really do. You help me be at my best, more of the time!' And he's so right.

I believe that at the centre of this 'leadership stuff' is you being At Your Best, More of the Time. And in turn helping others be the same.

I've learned that if I can help you spend more of your time, in more situations, being At Your Best, so much of your leading will then flow naturally. When you're at your most confident best, you're powerfully in touch with the Future you want and not held back by the present. You're more engaging and it's easier for people to feel they want to work with you. And you're much more likely to have the focus, drive and straight conversations needed for others to deliver.

This also shows up in your Energies. Your spirits are up and you are more inclined to connect emotionally with others. Your thinking is sharper and you have the Physical Energy to make things happen.

These are all pretty good reasons why you might want to be At Your Best, More of the Time — but there is a huge extra one if you're looking to lead others. It's that how you are is contagious!

If you're At Your Best, there's a better chance that those around you will be too. If you're down, flat or irritated, then there's a very good chance you can drag others down there with you – this is the power of your Light and Shadow.

It's exactly what Drucker was pointing to in his quote about energies – he asks you first to manage your own energy because it can have such a massive impact on those you want great energy from.

So that's the focus of this chapter – to help you be able to choose to spend more of your time At Your Best. Unlike other chapters, it doesn't introduce another aspect of leading. Rather, it's here to add depth and power to every aspect of your leadership. So let's see how you can manage yourself better to be 'At Your Best, More of the Time'.

> "In most management books, articles, and courses there is little or no importance placed on how you have to 'be' in order to excel at something. The typical management seminar is more likely to lead to colourful plastic binders than to an alteration of a person's way of being."
> Robert Hargrove

The overview

Here's the big picture: one way of looking at yourself is that you are a walking bundle of factors, including feelings, beliefs and energies. Some of these factors are the source of your magic and brilliance; some hold you back and limit you. It looks like this:

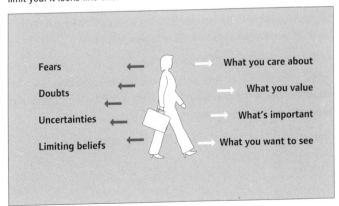

Fears

Doubts

Uncertainties

Limiting beliefs

What you care about

What you value

What's important

What you want to see

On the right is what takes you forward in life and has you At Your Best. It's the connection you have to what you care about, what's important to you, what you're committed to, what you value, what you're up to. These factors give you determination, persistence, resilience and staying power.

But at the same time, within you are doubts, fears and uncertainties which will take you away from being At Your Best – you're not the only one with the voice in your head giving you reasons why you can't do this or you're not good enough for that!

In any moment of time, how you are and what you're like is being shaped either by the forces on the right – what you care about, are committed to – or those on the left – your doubts, fears and limiting beliefs.

There's good and bad news about these disabling doubts, fears and beliefs. The bad news is that they don't ever really go away. The enormously good news is that you can significantly loosen their grip.

The way to loosen this grip is to take on two Conscious Practices.

The first is to be aware in any moment of who you're being and whether it's who you want to be. And the second is to choose who you want to be. It's as simple – but sometimes, not as easy – as that!

I can tell you from my personal experience that these can be life-changing practices. Why? Because there will be times in your life when you will be negatively triggered by people and situations. What you can learn to do is be triggered less and, when you are, return to your best sooner.

For instance, I can tell you that I used to spend about 60 per cent of my time feeling good, and 40 per cent worrying, doubtful or feeling afraid. With the help of the ideas in this chapter and some Conscious Practice, I'd say I'm now at my best around 90 per cent of my time.

You can make the same sort of shift. Here are the steps to take:

1 'At Your Best' versus 'Just Surviving'

First, think about how you'd describe people when they're At Their Best or when we might say they are Playing to Win in life, at home or at work. Add your words to these that others have used …

Now, imagine that moment when life's going fine and then you get that awful phone call, or you hear some really bad news. Instantly, you may feel your stomach turning or your mouth dry. You've just been triggered and now you're in Just Surviving mode – your focus now is not on a glorious Playing to Win; the focus now becomes Avoiding Losing.

Just Surviving has a completely different feel and would be described with different words. Add your own to these that others have used …

Defeated **Isolated** Helpless
Foolish Exposed Anxious
Defensive
Victim Fuming
Argumentative
Disengaged
Withdrawn Angry

And this is what we're all like. We each have these two different modes. There are moments when we are connected to what we care about and we feel good. And times when we are triggered into our fears and doubts. So how do we choose to be who we want to be? The first step is to heighten our self-awareness and notice what we're like.

When I took on the practice to be more conscious many years ago, I soon noticed that both my At My Best and Just Surviving modes came in two different flavours. I noticed that I had high-energy and low-energy versions.

For example, at home I noticed that I could sometimes be triggered by my son, Alex, into my high-energy Just Surviving version. I'd be angry and even aggressive – certainly not the way I wanted to be with him. In contrast, when I was triggered around my wife, Sharron, I was much more likely to slide into a low-energy Just Surviving mode where I was withdrawn and just wanting to get out of the room!

Exploring this territory with many others has revealed that we all have both these ways of being. And here's why. At times all of us want to be right and we want to feel safe. So in my high-energy survivor mode it's really all about attacking in order to defend. I'll do whatever it takes to be right. And at times I'll even look for that short-term rush from making others wrong! I don't want to be in this mode but I have learned that at times when I am triggered I want to be in control and if that means fighting about the detail of an argument, I'll fight.

Of course, I cast a big Shadow when I'm in this mode. Indeed I've been told very clearly by people in my Support Team that they can feel attacked, used, powerless, made wrong and inadequate at such times.

In contrast, in my low-energy mode, I'm basically afraid. I want to avoid interaction and get out. Sometimes, I feel as though I'll be safer by being liked. So I'll overdo being nice, deferential or agreeable just to achieve this end.

And here too my Impact Felt is not the one intended. People tell me they wonder, 'Where's Steve gone? Why's he so quiet? What's going on?' They are left confused, disconnected from me and at times feeling lost or alone.

So once I noticed that these were high- and low-energy versions of my Just Surviving mode I began to ask myself, 'What are the equivalent versions of me At My Best?' The answer here is that my high-energy version of me at my best is a 'Making it Happen' mode. I'm alive, with my Energies switched on. I'm up to something and moving things forward. I'm game for a laugh, and people feel engaged, energised, stretched and with their Physical Energy ready for action.

As for my low-energy version of being At My Best, this is where my energy is calm. I feel peaceful, reflective and can more easily be a leader who sits back and sees the bigger picture. This is also where I find my grace under pressure so I can respond more calmly to setbacks. People around me can feel included, listened to, even special. They can reconnect with what they care about and be inspired for what's next. Here, the Emotional and Spirit Energies can feel strong.

Now this is important, really important! The world is already fast and is still speeding up. As a result, life can be a non-stop stream of meetings, phone calls and e-mails. And I see more and more leaders struggling to find quiet time and calm energy.

As a leader, you have to create the time to stand back, see and embrace the big picture, the whole – this is critical to you developing your Future Leadership Muscles.

That's why I say you have to consciously plan for quiet time in your diary. And recognise that you probably won't get any encouragement to do this. Indeed your organisation, your boss and your colleagues will put pressure on you to be busy or to be in high-energy 'Make it Happen' mode. But some of the best leaders I've worked with also know how to pause regularly and see the big picture.

So notice yourself now.

- How great are you at finding quiet, thoughtful time?
- If you've not been great, why is that?
- What could you do to find that quiet time regularly?

Bringing all this together looks like this:

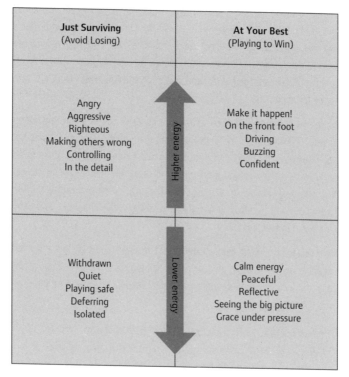

Just Surviving (Avoid Losing)	At Your Best (Playing to Win)
Angry Aggressive Righteous Making others wrong Controlling In the detail	Make it happen! On the front foot Driving Buzzing Confident
Withdrawn Quiet Playing safe Deferring Isolated	Calm energy Peaceful Reflective Seeing the big picture Grace under pressure

Higher energy

Lower energy

You spend time in each of the four boxes. Take some time now to describe yourself in each box. Feel great when writing words that describe you At Your Best. And be really honest in writing the words that describe what you're like when you're Just Surviving. (Use the chart here or print off one at **www.futureengagedeliver.com/book**. You'll also find pages for the next questions there too.)

> "The greatest discovery of any generation is that human beings can alter their lives by altering their attitudes of mind."
>
> Albert Schweitzer

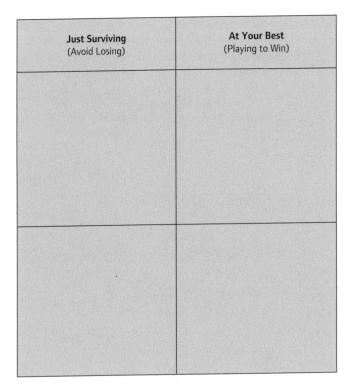

Just Surviving (Avoid Losing)	At Your Best (Playing to Win)

2 Your Impact Intended and Impact Felt

Now you've described what you're like in each of the four boxes, I'd like you to be clearer than ever about your impact on those around you. First, put into words the impact you'd like to have on others, your Impact Intended.

_____

_____

_____

_____

_____

Now write down words in each box which you imagine describe how people feel around you, i.e. do your best to describe your Impact Felt for each box. Think about the Light and Shadow you bring to people in and out of work and be as honest as you can.

Your Impact Felt	
Just Surviving (Avoid Losing)	**At Your Best** (Playing to Win)

Now you've done this, what do you see about yourself?

- In which box do you spend most of your time?
- Is the answer different at home and at work?
- In what situations are you more likely to be At Your Best or Just Surviving?
- How much do you allow yourself to rest in the bottom right 'calm' box?
- What do you see about how you'll come across as a leader in each box?
- How clearly can you see that you have a wide range of Impacts Felt?

- Where are you most Guided by the Future you Want?

- Where are you most Engaging?

- Where are you most likely to have others Deliver More Now?

- And where are you most likely to be developing them to Deliver More Later?

These questions are here to help you build your self-awareness as the first step to choosing who you want to be. You can deepen this awareness further by asking your Support Team to describe you and your impact. And you can deepen it further again by answering these next questions.

> "A leader is a person who has an unusual degree of power to project onto other people his or her shadow or his or her light ... A leader is a person who must take special responsibility for what is going on inside him or herself lest the act of leadership create more harm than good."
>
> Parker J Palmer

3 Your Triggers

Each of us has Triggers that knock us off being At Our Best – for example, I've talked above about Alex and Sharron. Something happens and instantly we're triggered and taken out and we are then governed by our fears and doubts. I encourage you to notice what your Triggers are. Look for them starting now and every day. That way, with practice, you can see them coming, pause and increasingly choose not to be triggered.

I've mentioned earlier that all sorts of different things will trigger you. Certain people or a type of person can trigger you. Or someone's tone of voice or how they look at you. You can be triggered by the thought of certain meetings and interactions. Or by people not doing what you want or how you'd do it. The list goes on.

The key is to notice these Triggers. You may want to try and work out where they came from but this is less important than noticing them, and letting them go. Start writing your list of Triggers here and add to it as you notice more of them.

_____

_____

Again, what do you notice about yourself? What patterns do you see?

Having identified some of your Triggers, you can immediately put this awareness to use. Just rest for a while and imagine situations where you are triggered; think about them and make them as real as you can. Then imagine you being At Your Best in those situations; imagine yourself not triggered.

You may only be able to imagine yourself being triggered and then regathering yourself and being who you want to be. That's fine. What would that look like in these situations? How would you feel? What would you say? How would you speak?

You can practise this visualisation now and ahead of situations where you think you may be triggered. Imagine going into that situation At Your Best, watching the trigger arrive and staying At Your Best. You may surprise yourself with how powerful this practice can be.

> "The art of resting the mind and the power of dismissing from it all care and worry is probably one of the secrets of energy in our great men."
>
> J A Hadfield

4 Your Costs

To help you be stronger at choosing who you want to be it's also helpful to be in touch with the costs of going into your Just Surviving mode.

This is a section to do thoroughly if you want to grow as fast as possible as a leader. Yes, you'll grow as a leader through your Conscious Practice and by building your Leadership Muscles, but a single interaction where you are in Just Surviving mode can undo a lot of your good work.

You may not be able to see these costs fully yet but I can promise you that they are significant. There'll be a number of costs to you when you're Just Surviving. Have a think now about what some of them could be before I tell you what I commonly hear.

_____

_____

_____

_____

Most costs fall under two broad headings: your energy and your relationships. Too much time Just Surviving and your energy will be poor. This is how you bring on stress, get seriously tired, drain yourself. Second, when you're in surviving mode you can be driving your relationships backwards, making them smaller.

This isn't great news for anyone but it's of particular importance if you want to lead. So let's look again at *Future–Engage–Deliver* and the Four Energies to see some of the costs of Just Surviving.

> "Our deepest fear is not that we are inadequate. Our deepest fear is that we are powerful beyond measure."
>
> Marianne Williamson

Future

When you're Just Surviving, your focus is not on the glorious Future you want. It's more on 'how do I survive now?' There is little sense of energising possibilities. It's more about 'how do I get out of this hole?' There's no strong sense of being up to something. You may be deep in the details of your Operator Mode.

Engage

When you're at your engaging best, you're connected with others and you're working with them. When you're Just Surviving, your primary focus is on you. This can leave people disengaged from you. At worst, you will alienate people and drive them away from you. They can feel attacked, put down, worthless – hardly the characteristics of a Big Relationship!

Deliver

At Your Best, you bring focus, energy and high standards to Deliver. In Just Surviving, you may not bring any focus or energy. You may have withdrawn and gone quiet. Others can then conclude that you didn't really want what you're asking for. And as they'll all have other things to do too, they may not follow through on your priorities.

Alternatively, you bring lots of energy but it's used to blame and attack others, make them wrong and undermine their energy and self-belief. Be clear, this is not Robust Dialogue. In your high-energy surviving mode, you can force people to deliver for a while. But they won't offer their best over the long term for someone dealing with them this way.

> "Those parts you're unaware of will make your choices for you. You cannot choose intentions consciously until you become conscious of each of the different aspects of yourself."
>
> Gary Zukav

The Four Energies

You can probably imagine the impact Just Surviving has on the Energies. When you're surviving, you're probably dispiriting yourself and others. There may be low Emotional Energy because people don't care. Or there may be lots of Emotional Energy but it's of a negative, complaining sort. There may be Intellectual and Physical Energies but they're focused only on getting out of this situation; they're not linked to a Spirit Energy about a compelling Future.

I hope you're getting a sense that the costs to you of your Just Surviving mode are high.

To put it bluntly, when you're in this mode you are working directly against what you care about and are leading for.

You can spend ages At Your Best being the leader you want to be. And much of your good work can be undone by just a moment in Just Surviving. And to add more, there will also be times when there are costs that come even when you're At Your Best.

Helen was a really capable leader who wanted to leave people energised and full of possibilities; that was her Impact Intended. She spent most of her work time in high-energy At Your Best mode but her energy was too high for others and they didn't feel in touch with her; they'd say she seemed on a different plane, didn't listen to them or try to take them with her. So when you're feeling good and your energy is high, just pause now and again. Make sure people are with you.

Which brings us nicely to the final point on costs – don't try to work them out by yourself; use your Support Team. They can tell you better than you can what some of the costs are to you when you're in Just Surviving mode.

> "We learn by letting go of all the negative thoughts that clutter our minds with fear. A wise man knows that he has only one enemy – himself. This is an enemy difficult to ignore and full of cunning. It assails one with doubts and fears."
>
> Ben Hecht

5 How You Benefit

Interestingly, while there are real costs to you when you're Just Surviving, there are also benefits. How do you benefit from being in Just Surviving mode? How do you gain from your high-energy, attacking mode? And how from withdrawing and going quiet? Again, before I tell you what I've found out, take a minute to think what they may be for you.

_____

_____

_____

_____

As I suggested earlier, some of the benefits of Just Surviving are that you get to be right and to feel safer. In high-energy mode, you protect yourself by doing whatever you can to feel right and keep others at bay, including making them wrong. That way, you feel safer. In low-energy mode, you pull away from what feels like attack or threat from others, and thereby protect yourself and feel safer.

However, this is not a deep feeling of safety. It's a short-term, perceived benefit to get you by but not one that has you feeling really good. Deeper down, you still feel tense, anxious, defensive or afraid. Your behaviour is trying to help you but it's not addressing how you really feel.

So you can get a short-term benefit from your surviving mode but the question to you is, 'Does the perceived benefit outweigh the costs?' Yes, you can feel the perverse sense of strength from making others wrong. Or the relief of avoiding conflict or argument. But are these benefits more important to you than the costs of setting back your relationships, weakening your energy and thereby holding you back as a leader?

> "Ninety per cent of the world's woe comes from people not knowing themselves, their abilities, their frailties, and real virtues. Most of us go through life as complete strangers to ourselves."
>
> Sidney Harris

6 Getting Back to Being At Your Best

So what more can you do about all this? The first step is to be better at quickly getting out of your Just Surviving mode and back to being At Your Best. You already have ways of doing this. I'd like to extend your list and encourage more Conscious Practice.

One way of returning to your best is to practise seeing the bigger picture and putting things into perspective. You can do this by having a break, going for a walk, getting some exercise or sleeping on it. You can think about the bigger picture of your life and view the current situation from there – i.e. is what your struggling with, or have been triggered by, as important as your health or family or friends?

Some of this you can do alone. Sometimes, contact with others makes the difference. You might get back to being At Your Best after you've talked your issue through with a colleague or friend. You might just want to let off steam for a while, or feel listened to. You might want to lighten up with some social time. Here is where we all need a Support Team.

The other practice is to be Guided by the Future you Want and here's how it can help you be At Your Best. Think again about the diagram of you as that walking bundle of positive values and energies to the right and fears and doubts to the left. When you're Just Surviving, you're being governed by your fears and doubts. So shift to being guided by those forces pulling you the other way. You can do this by reconnecting with your answers to the three big questions I asked in Chapter 3:

- What do you care about?
- What do you want to lead for? and
- Who is the leader you want to be?

These are the rocks on which your leadership stands. If you have powerful answers to these questions, however you're feeling, you can pause and get in touch with these drivers. This can be an immensely powerful practice. It's one of my personal favourites and one I've called on many times over the years.

Which leads us nicely to the final thought of this chapter …

> "The best thing you can do is get good at being you."
>
> Dennis the Menace

7 Practising Being At Your Best, More of the Time

Finally, there is one more way of being At Your Best, More of the Time. Rather than wait for a tough situation to come along and some Trigger to take you out, prepare ahead of time. Think about any situations where you are not At Your Best. Write down a list of them. Make them specific – in which situations, with which people, in which meetings, etc.

_____

_____

_____

_____

_____

Then flex your Imagining Muscles and picture yourself At Your Best in each of those situations. Picture how you would feel, how your energy would be. Imagine the Trigger that previously grabbed you and be clear on how you'd respond if you were At Your Best. Don't wait until the moment arrives and be caught out. Imagine it all ahead of time. Build your ability to choose who you want to be. Give yourself the very best chance of being the person and leader you want to be.

> "The wise leader knows what is happening by being aware of what is happening here and now. This is more potent than wandering off into various theories. By staying present and aware of what is happening, the leader can do less yet achieve more."
>
> John Heider

In summary …

So what's the message? It's that we can all spend more time being who we want to be. Put more fully, we can all spend more time being the leader we want to be, in touch with the Future we care about, engaging others to build it with us and working alongside them to deliver it efficiently and at pace.

The underlying Leadership Muscles I've encouraged you to build through practice are Awareness and Choice. If you want to have more impact as a leader, you need to be more conscious of what's going on around you and crucially become more aware of who you are being in every moment. This gives you the chance of choosing to be at your best in that moment.

Enjoy the benefits of building these Muscles. Do it through Conscious Practice and with your Support Team by your side.

And now, let's turn to how you can bring everything we've looked at to the teams you are in.

FED IN PRACTICE

MARTIN CARTER

Martin Carter is a Director of Health, Safety & Environment and explains here how showing up at his best starts with awareness of his own mindset.

'They say leaders should tell stories. Well, I want to encourage you to tell fewer stories! I'm not talking about inspirational leadership stories that help engage others in what you are up to. I'm talking about the corrosive internal stories we tell ourselves about our limitations, shortcomings and weaknesses.

'I surprised myself a while ago when, in a meeting with two more senior colleagues whom I greatly respect and admire, I suddenly found myself admitting that I couldn't quite believe that I kept getting away with it – by which I meant securing bigger roles which I believed needed a far more diligent, talented and capable professional than me to do them. I finished by saying, "I just try and get to the end of each day without being found out." My honesty shocked, but not as much as their reply. They both looked at me and said, "What, you too? I thought that was just me!"

'Superficially, the exchange was light-hearted but in that moment we all recognised we were revealing a deeply held, darkly feared truth about ourselves.

'I didn't have the language of FED at the time, but I see now that the stories we were telling ourselves had us consistently playing to Avoid Losing – to not get "found out". These days, I've been working hard at not listening to that internal story and instead concentrating on Playing to Win and trusting that, regardless of what the internal voice might say, turning up at my best will be good enough … and if it's not? Well if it didn't work out when I turned up at my best, it definitely wouldn't have worked out if I didn't!'

Future–Engage–
Deliver and **Teams**

… in short, you've got to be 'up to something together'.

- Future–Engage–Deliver and **Teams**
- Finding the initial spark
- 'Future' and Teams
  - The importance of 'The Gap'
  - The Gap Plus
- 'Engage' and Teams
  - When Engagement's missing
- 'Deliver' and Teams
  - Deliver through Others
  - Deliver More Now
  - Deliver More Later
  - Putting it all into Practice: The Leader's Conversations for Delivery

Future–Engage–Deliver and Teams

Here, I want to focus on how you can show up as a leader in that special arena we call 'teams'. Teams are a brilliant lever to help you build the Future You Want even faster. But most people I work with tell me they spend hours and hours in team meetings that are seriously unproductive and draining. I find it remarkable that these capable people don't know what to focus on and what to do to make teams and meetings much more energising and productive.

The very short version of *Future–Engage–Deliver* and Teams is that most teams:

- do way too little Future and Engage,
- leave lots of Emotional and Spirit Energy untapped and unused,
- have too many members in Operator/Manager Mode, and so are left trying to do lots of Deliver without properly preparing the ground.

So the aim of this chapter is to help you see what's going on in teams that work and what's missing in teams that don't. I'll then help you identify what practices you can take on to help teams perform closer to their potential. Crucially, I want to help you get teams you are in to work regardless of whether you are the formal leader or one of the players. Again, I want to release us all from the old story that there is one leader and lots of followers. I want to encourage the mindset that we can all be leaders at any time regardless of our position or title.

This one chapter on teams will give you everything you need to raise your game because again all you need are a few big ideas and lots of practice and muscle building. You will discover here:

- how to use *Future–Engage–Deliver* in teams,
- how the Four Energies are a powerful way of seeing and then influencing what's happening in a team, and
- the benefits of having you and your team members At Your Best More of the Time.

Finding the initial spark

Yes, I'm here again, sitting in a room with a group of capable, experienced people and they are plodding! They have done their pre-reading, they have a clear agenda, they are pleasant with each other but there is absolutely no spark. They are all in Operator/Manager Mode and no one is enjoying the meeting. I let them know that this is my read of the situation and they all agree. So they all know it's not working but they're doing nothing to change it!

Two hours later, the situation is dramatically different. It started with my invitation to Sophie, the formal leader of the group, to talk about what she was up to as a leader. This brought her out of Operator/Manager Mode, she spoke from the heart and brought the Emotional and Spirit Energies that had been totally missing. This sparked off others to see what they could be up to and so the sense of possibility and excitement grew.

Within a short time, they had in the room the one ingredient I help teams have more than any other – they had a growing sense of the magic team ingredient,

"We Are Up To Something Together."

That is, there is a strong sense of team members being committed to a Future and engaged with each other. This is the ingredient I always look for first when I meet any team. I have learned that when this ingredient is present, any topic can get sorted with pace. When it's missing, virtually any small matter can hold a team back and delay progress – to paraphrase an old quote, 'In the absence of shared vision, pettiness prevails!'

If you take only one thought from this chapter, take this one. If you can find ways of helping grow this sense in your teams, they will amaze you. If this team spirit stays missing, it'll be hard work.

So check in on yourself now:

- When you have been in a team that has been 'up to something together', what has it felt like and how well did it perform?

- What helped this key ingredient to be present?

- What teams have you been in that did not have this characteristic and how did they perform?

- What do you notice you did and didn't do to help improve these teams' performance?

- And crucially, what do you see from this perspective about the teams you are in now?

Now let me help you see how you can help a group of people create and maintain this energising sense of 'We Are Up To Something Together'. Not surprisingly, it involves each of Future, Engage and Deliver:

- **Future** is where the 'Something' is co-invented,

- **Engage** is where 'Together' is cemented, and

- **Deliver** is where the 'Something' is made real through working 'Together'.

> "Keep away from people who belittle your ambitions. Small people always do that, but the really great make you feel that you, too, can become great."
>
> Mark Twain

'Future' and Teams

I'll always remember an excellent day I spent with a board team of a major organisation helping them explore their Future. It started with lots of Intellectual Energy in the room. It didn't feel particularly safe and the conversation was dry and lifeless.

I decided we needed a change of gear so I said, *'Ok, we are going to do something different now. I want you to go outside and sit alone for 20 minutes and write down your answers to two questions. They are,* "What do you care about?" *and* "What is the future organisation you'd be proud to help build, i.e. what do you want to lead for?" *I then want you to come back in and share your answers with your colleagues.'*

I had steered them into an exploration of the Future, exactly in line with the big ideas in the earlier chapter. When they returned I then requested, *'Each of you please share your answers but the question I want you all to answer when everyone has finished is,* "What did you hear the group say?"'

That is, I wanted them to search for the ideas about the Future that they heard and they all wanted. They did brilliantly.

> *They each spoke bringing Emotional and Spirit Energies and they completely surprised themselves to find that they were much more aligned than they'd ever realised.*

Very quickly they then summarised this strong sense of alignment in just three simple ideas that captured the organisation's new direction and purpose. This was an example of Co-invention at its best.

As I explained earlier, the Future aspect of leading is about being in touch with the Future you want to see. One of the first jobs for a team is to search for the common ground among the players, not the differences, and so discover the Future, the 'cathedral', they want to build together. It can be phrased as a 'shared goal, purpose, mission, aspiration' and it will be strongest when that team Future embraces and encourages what each player is up to.

Notice now:

- How strong is the sense of a shared Future in your teams?
- If it's present, what can you do to make sure it stays present?
- If it's missing, how might you start a conversation that helps the team build a sense of shared Future?

Now back to this team. They were off to a great start but I've learned the hard way that helping a team align just on the Future is not enough. They also have to align on the size of 'The Gap'. Let me explain.

> "To give up the bird in the hand, a company must see a dozen birds in the bush. The future must become just as vivid and real as the present and the past. Senior management must help the organisations build an intellectually compelling and emotionally enticing view of the future."
>
> Hamel and Prahalad

The importance of 'The Gap'

In another session many years ago, I helped a team agree that they wanted to be the best organisation of their kind in Europe. But something didn't feel right. It didn't feel as if they were 'together'. I didn't know what was going on until I asked the question, *'So how big is The Gap between this Future You Want and where you are today?'*

Immediately, there were two very different answers in the room. The established members of the board believed they were already very nearly the best in Europe. The new members believed they were miles away.

That was when I learned that for groups to be truly 'up to something together' they not only need a shared view of the Future They Want but also a shared view of three characteristics of The Gap:

1   Size
2   Commitment
3   Urgency

Here's how it looks:

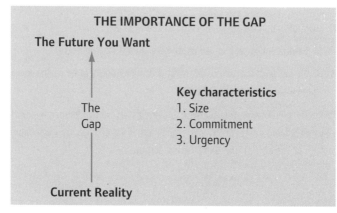

THE IMPORTANCE OF THE GAP

The Future You Want

The
Gap

Current Reality

Key characteristics
1. Size
2. Commitment
3. Urgency

1 Size

The perceived size of The Gap between Current Reality and Future You Want massively shapes the approach brought by a team to closing The Gap.

If the size of The Gap is small and asks for only incremental change, people can assume they just need to do a bit more of what they're already doing so don't stretch themselves or others. But if the size of The Gap is perceived as great, it can create a completely different mindset.

It can spark uncharacteristic challenge to current norms, it can foster breakthrough thinking and be the catalyst for whole new levels of creativity and innovation.

So the job here for a team is not only to have a conversation about the Future but also one about the Current Reality. Again this will require listening for the common ground and encouraging a shared understanding of where you are now so that you build a sense of alignment on the size of The Gap.

> "A demanding performance challenge tends to create a team. The hunger for performance is far more important to team success than special incentives or team leaders with ideal profiles."
> Katzenbach and Smith

2 Commitment

I've seen lots of individuals participate in these conversations in an academic, even detached, sort of way. That very often isn't enough. It's important to reveal in teams how engaged each of the players is. If people are in Resistance, Apathy or Grudging Compliance, get this said. You will move fastest when the players are Enrolled or, ideally, Committed. As I'll say more about in a while, have the conversations to help team members move up the Levels of Engagement. This may take more time up front but the investment will pay back many times over from the added pace later on.

3 Urgency

And finally, notice that while all players may be committed to the Future they may not see it as urgent. I'm committed to going to Alaska to take photographs but it's not urgent; I'll go in a few years' time. Again, you need to know where the team players stand.

So pause for a while and think about your teams and these aspects of The Gap.

- How sure are you that all the players see the same size of Gap?

- How committed do your colleagues seem? How could you get to know for sure?

- How urgent would you like colleagues to be compared with how they seem?

- What would it look like if you were sparking conversations to help people get this clear and so build alignment even further?

The Gap Plus

You can now deepen even further the team's sense of being 'up to something together' by building on The Gap model.

You can do this by having the team answer a number of questions. A typical running order is:

1 **Priorities**

2 **Culture**

3 **Team Ways of Working**

4 **Team and Individual Development**

5 **Next Steps**

Let's take each in turn.

1 Priorities

So given the Future We Want and the size of The Gap, what are the tangible aspects of the organisation that we must focus on now?

For instance, the answer may be customer relationships, service quality, patient waiting time, recruitment, pupil behaviour, new sales channels, talent management, etc.

Whatever your answer, these are the most important banners under which you will start creating a different Future.

At times the banners are obvious. At other times, this requires detailed strategy work but don't make it more complicated than it needs to be.

2 Culture

To create the Future We Want, what culture will we need in the organisation and how different will that be from the one we have today?

It's important that a team understands whether it's possible to build the new Future inside the current culture or whether a new culture is needed. Ambitious breakthrough Futures will most likely demand a new culture. It's better to identify this up front rather than create processes and set goals which simply won't happen because the current culture will strangle them.

Of course, creating a new culture is a major challenge and takes time. Be honest with yourselves about what's needed, what values must be lived in the team and beyond and at the very least start living them in the team. Which leads us to …

> "The bottom line for leaders is that if they do not become conscious of the cultures in which they are embedded, those cultures will manage them. Cultural understanding is desirable for all of us, but it is essential to leaders if they are to lead."
>
> Ed Schein

3 Team Ways of Working

Given the above answers, who is the team we want to be and how will we work together?

A big question from the Future chapter is, 'Who is the Leader you want to be?' Get your team to answer the same question about the team. Then move to how it will look working together brilliantly. Get clear on the roles people will play.

Be clear on who is responsible for what. Agree the practical stuff – how often we'll meet, for how long to cover what, how we'll work between meetings. And be clear on the behaviours that will be needed to accelerate performance.

Yes, this all sounds pretty obvious but so often I see teams leap into the 'what' and spend little time on the 'how'.

What are your teams like in this regard? And what extra could you do to have them be much clearer on who the team wants to be and how you'll work together?

> "It's easy to get good players. Getting them to play together, that's the hard part."
>
> Casey Stengel

4 Team and Individual Development

How will we need to grow both as a team and individually to pull all this off?

Sometimes a team can pull off what it's up to within its current capabilities. In which case, fine. Often, though, a team will need to make a leap in its development and this needs to be talked about explicitly and worked on. The earlier question of, 'Who is the team we want to be?' can really help here. Answering this question can then lead you on to, 'So how do we need to grow to become that team?' Make the topic explicit.

You can accelerate this growth further by then adding the next question … 'So to grow like this as a team, how might each of us need to grow individually?' That is, accelerate team growth by having each of the players take on growing themselves as leaders and mutually supporting each other.

> "The greatest danger a team faces isn't that it won't become successful, but that it will, and then cease to improve."
>
> Mark Sanborn

5 Next Steps

What do we need to do next to build further momentum?

That is, bring in the Physical Energy and be clear on what you're going to do next and by when.

Pause here and think of your teams:

- Which of these questions do you have clear and energising answers to?
- What's your mental picture of you At Your Best being a catalyst for all questions getting answered? How would you feel, speak and engage?

By the time you have helped a team cover this ground, there should be good Spirit Energy, a strong sense of Future, a picture of the 'something' the team want to be 'up to together' and some ideas about how they are going to do it. Unfortunately, many teams labour together without this sense of Future. Instead they bury themselves in Deliver where it feels like forever carving stone without a sense of purpose.

I've touched on the need to have team members be sufficiently engaged to bring their energy to these Future conversations. This is not always the case and there are three ways in particular you can have Engage live strongly in your teams.

> "One of the simple pleasures of Great Groups is that they are almost never bureaucratic. People in them feel liberated from the trivial and the arbitrary."
>
> Warren Bennis

'Engage' and Teams

It's in the Engage aspect of leading that you ensure it's in a 'together' way that the team is up to something.

However, I'd say that it's in this Engage space that most teams are weakest and let themselves down.

I can make this instantly clear by looking at the *Relationships to Results Pyramid* we saw in Chapter 4. I use this framework all the time when working with teams. Here it is again.

Results

Actions Physical

Opportunities, Priorities Intellectual

Possibilities, Ideas Spirit

Relationships Emotional

Unfortunately, this isn't the shape when teams work below their potential. It's actually more like this:

Results

Actions Physical

Opportunities, Priorities Intellectual

Possibilities, Ideas Spirit

Relationships Emotional

That is, many teams give lots of time and energy to the planning of Priorities and identifying of Actions without attending to the foundation aspects of

Relationships and Future Possibilities. Put another way, they are full of Intellectual and Physical Energies and don't unlock and harness the potentially more powerful Emotional and Spirit Energies.

The result is that teams may put in all the hours they want but still be held back by the fact that team members aren't all strongly engaged and excited by the Future – not enough Future and Engage and so ineffective Deliver.

What's your view of your teams?

- What has your team done to ensure each player is engaged rather than in Compliance, Apathy or Resistance?
- How does it welcome and build relationships with new members? Or is the assumption that they will be engaged from day one?
- How positively strong are the Emotional and Spirit Energies? To what extent are they consciously managed?
- How well do your teams bring out the best in you and help you grow?
- How well do they encourage you to be in Leader Mode? Probably well when you're the formal leader, but what about when you're not?
- Put in simple terms, do you and others feel valued, included and do you have fun?

When Engagement's missing

Over the years, I've identified three ways engagement can be often missing from teams. Notice their relevance to your teams and what you could do to make sure they're addressed.

1 Team members are insufficiently engaged in the team

It was pretty clear that Gary, the supply chain member of a global team, was not fully engaged in the team. I asked him how he was doing and he said he was struggling because this was the fifth team he was in and he couldn't give his all to every one of them. He was already a member of local site, country, regional and functional teams and he felt the global team was a step too far.

But when we talked a little further, the deeper reason behind his disengagement became clear. In contrast to all his other teams, he didn't feel valued in this one, i.e. he didn't have a big enough Relationship with the team. So far we have pointed to the importance of Relationships with people.

For teams to perform, it's also important to build people's Relationship to the team.

Gary with five teams is an extreme example but it applies to all of us. We want to feel valued, to know that we matter, to be listened to and to know our opinion counts. In his other teams, Gary felt the power of this Emotional Energy. In this one, he felt taken for granted. This is a particular challenge for teams geographically spread or working in a virtual way but it's a challenge I believe must be addressed by taking the time to have people feel included and valued.

Notice for yourself:

- In what teams have you felt valued?
- In what teams have you not?
- How do you feel in your current teams?
- How well is the Emotional Energy freed and used?
- How valued do you think your team colleagues feel?
- What have you noticed helps people feel valued and what can work against this?

This is all about the bottom box of the Pyramid. It wasn't big enough for Gary with the global team. The good news is that, once this was spoken about, a much deeper relationship-building conversation took place. Gary became a much stronger team member and felt 'together' with the team.

2 Team members are not engaged in each other

The interdependent way of working in teams calls for Big Relationships between the players. The size of Relationships in a team can be a major drag on or a real accelerator of performance. Yet they are often not consciously worked on. Here is the standard to aim for if you really want your teams to fly.

My experience, backed by others' research, is that in high-performing teams the members are not only committed to the success of the team, they are also committed to the success of each other.

That is, you not only want the team to win, you also want each of your colleagues to be at their best and succeed. This makes for a truly strong bottom box of the Pyramid and Possibilities in the next box up will seem enormous.

This may not be a common ingredient in your relationships. What do you see?

- Who is committed to your success? In the past, you may have had a teacher, family friend, boss in an early job, etc. but who do you have now?

- How good does it feel when you have someone committed to your success?

- Whose success are you committed to?

- Who does that include on your teams and who does it not include?

- What might it look like if you were committed to all your team members' success?

- And what do you see might be possible if this were a common feature of all relationships in the team?

You might use the Pyramid to introduce this idea into your teams. I have found that this basis for a relationship has been very powerful for me. It's live every day in my interactions with work colleagues. It is the basis on which we commit to relationships with clients.

However, one thing to notice is whose definition of success you are steering by. As my dear wife, Sharron, made clear to me a few years ago, *'Steve, I'm pleased you want me to succeed but it needs to be my definition of success, not yours!'* It's an important distinction that I haven't forgotten since! So don't just get to know your team colleagues. Get to know what success would be for them – as defined by them.

> "The true high-performance team is rare. This is largely because a high degree of personal commitment to one another differentiates people on high-performance teams from people on other teams."
>
> Katzenbach and Smith

3 Members are engaged as Leaders of a Part not Leaders of the Whole

The dynamics of many teams often quietly encourage members to be in passive Operator/Manager Mode rather than in fully participating Leader Mode. And even when people are in Leader Mode, they are only Leader of a Part, i.e. they bring themselves as the head of their part, their department, their function. At worst, several players being Leaders of a Part starts turf-wars, turns departments into silos, and means the 'barons' will do anything to protect their patch. This is not teamwork at its best!

This is why encouraging team members to be owners or Leaders of the Whole can be so powerful.

When you are a Leader of the Whole, your main focus is having the whole team succeed rather than just your part.

This is quite a different mindset. You enjoy seeing others succeed. You're more likely to make sacrifices for the common good. You'll bring more energy to collaborating with colleagues. And potentially you'll make a much bigger difference.

This shift of mindset to owning the whole is extremely powerful. But in teams I'm invited to work with it rarely seems to be spoken about. What's the story in your teams?

- In which teams have you been a Leader of a Part and in which a Leader of the Whole? In particular, what do you see about the role you play in current teams?

- Which of your team colleagues would you say are Leaders of a Part? And which are Leaders of the Whole?

- What do you see is possible if everyone stepped into being Leaders of the Whole?

- What conversations could you start that would help people shift there?

So in summary, here are three aspects of engagement to look out for inside your teams. Do all you can to make sure team members are:

- engaged in the team,

- engaged in each other to a high level, and

- are showing up as Leaders of the Whole.

This way you'll have a fully shaped Pyramid from Relationships to Results and you are ready to move to another space of Engage, the engaging of others outside the team.

> "Owners think differently from non-owners because ownership is a state of mind. It's about caring. Non-owners may be more inclined to pursue self-interest. Owners transcend functional boundaries."
>
> Lissack and Roos

Engagement beyond the team

Everything I wrote in Chapter 4 on Engage now applies to your engagement of others. A team can rarely achieve its ambition without the active, ongoing and planned engagement of others. Take all the ideas from the Engage chapter and bring them to your team conversation. Identify together:

- Who do we need to engage to pull off what we are up to?

- At which Level of Engagement is each of them now?

- What Level do we want them to be?

- Who in the team will be assigned to engage whom, how and by when? and

- How will we monitor the progress we make?

For some teams, this planning takes on the feel of a campaign charted out with a timeline and names attached. Even further, there may be conversations to have in the team to help each player be a confident, engaging ambassador for what you are up to together. Get aligned and get your messages clear. Support each other to be at your engaging best. And celebrate your successes along the way.

This may sound over-thorough but I cannot underline enough how a proactive engagement plan and approach can add enormous pace and momentum to a team's performance. How thorough have your teams been here and what do you see might be possible from a more planned approach?

> "The person who figures out how to harness the collective creative genius of the people in his or her organisation is going to blow the competition away."
>
> Walter Wriston

'Deliver' and Teams

Deliver and Teams is essentially about applying everything in the Deliver chapter to the team setting. Let's review the main ideas with teams in mind.

Deliver through Others

Regardless of your role in a team, make sure you're choosing the mode you are in. At times you will need to be in Operator/Manager Mode but don't stay there. And when you choose to be in Leader Mode, be a Leader of the Whole. At times, you may just want to represent your specific part but at your best you will be stepping back and seeing the big picture. You'll be imagining and steering by what success is for the team, not just your part. Also you'll encourage others to bring the same mindset.

> "Great Groups continue to struggle until the project is brought to a successful conclusion. Great curiosity and problem-solving ability are not enough. There must also be continuous focus on the task until the work is done."
>
> Warren Bennis

Deliver More Now

1 To Deliver More Now, you must first have made a great job of Future and Engage

I've underlined this several times in this chapter. Too often, teams shoot straight to Deliver without preparing the ground. I'll always remember being alongside the new head of an organisation telling his board in their first meeting that such and such were the two priorities that they must deliver on. The swift reply from one of the team was, *'Would you like our comments or do you just want us to obey?'*

The new head took it well and asked me after the session how he could have handled it better. You'll know the summary of what I said – next time, build some Future together and Engage your new colleagues before moving to Deliver!

2 To excel in Deliver, you have to mean it!

Having a team consistently perform well is a large-scale exercise in focused energy management. All The Four Energies are present and all need managing – this is another reason to have more leaders in a team than just one; everyone can share the load.

I've worked for years with teams in one organisation where intellectual debate is enjoyed. It's the place I first heard the phrase, *'Once the decision's been made, that's when the debate begins!!'*

This is absolutely not good enough for a team who are up to something together. Such a team brings a different level of energy and has a different quality of conversation because they mean it. They have lively Robust Dialogue in which standards are high, issues are tabled, different points of view are expressed, big requests and promises are made, and decisions when taken are committed to.

Yes, both low- and high-performing teams may have clear goals, timelines, budgets and meeting agendas and minutes. But the high-performing teams have something extra.

They have an energy, a resolve and sense of possibility

that come from members being up to something together and meaning it.

- How do you describe the energy in your teams?
- What drains the energy and what raises it?
- If you were more of a Leader of the Whole, what extra could you do to help the team's energy and strengthen the sense of 'we mean it'?

There are two particular aspects of teams who mean it which are worth special mention. The first is the quality of the team members and how they perform. If you really want the team to succeed, you must have the right mix of skills and experience on the team. And there will be no room for passengers. Set your standards high when choosing team members and have Robust Dialogue with those who aren't performing.

The second is Early Wins and Symbols. One way to announce to yourselves and others that you mean it is to purposely get some Early Wins or take some overt, untypical decisions or actions which make people sit up and take notice. The added benefit here is that Early Wins are a powerful way to lift the energy and early confidence in the team.

So there are some ideas to help your team Deliver More Now but the best teams don't stop there. The best constantly look for how they can improve their teamplay in order to Deliver More Later.

> "When we are debating an issue, loyalty means giving me your honest opinion, whether you think I'll like it or not. Disagreement, at this stage, stimulates me. But once a decision has been made, the debate ends. From that point on, loyalty means executing the decision as if it were your own."
>
> Colin Powell

Deliver More Later

When we lived in America, it struck me that their sports had something in common. At times the game was stopped so the teams could talk about how they were currently playing and how they could change to play even better. This taking 'time out' seems such an effective way to maximise the chance of success. So why is it that most of the teams in organisations I've seen don't naturally do this?

It seems odd. Here is a way we could be smarter, but we usually don't use it! When a team is truly up to something together, it is constantly learning about what's working and what's not, and building on its successes.

From its work in the Future aspect of leading, the team is clear about 'who is the team we want to be?' It regularly checks in on whether they are being that way and how they can grow even more. Again, constructive Robust Dialogue is the order of the day.

And the team's capacity to deliver is developed another way too. It's through team members developing each other. Teams are a fine place for you to be At Your Best and do lots to help others be their best too.

This is the mindset of the Player/Coach – how can I play At My Best and encourage and guide others to be there too?

In the best teams, members are open with each other on 'who is the leader I want to be', how they are trying to grow and they actively seek feedback from others. This makes sense to me but I find it's uncommon. What's been your experience? Have you been in teams where this was the norm? If not, what got in the way of this way of working? And what could you do to start this dialogue?

Unfortunately, a common pattern of teams is to get fixated on the 'what' and lose sight of the 'how' – how are we playing as a team, how are we growing as a team, how are we doing helping each other be At Our Best?

Make sure the 'how' gets airtime. Don't put it as the last item of the agenda. Set aside serious time for how you can Deliver More Now and Deliver More Later.

> "I want people who arrive in the morning with a smile on their faces ready to take on the tasks of the day. They're going to create energy, and energise the people they work with."
>
> Larry Bossidy

Putting it all into Practice: The Leader's Conversations for Delivery

Finally, let me reinforce the idea that so much of the Deliver aspect of leading is shaped by the nature and quality of conversations in a team.

You can bring this alive by using The Leader's Conversations for Delivery framework as a self-assessment tool within the team. Consider having a session in which you take the team through the framework and talk about where you have been strong and weak, and how you might raise your game.

For instance, you might look at:

Conversation 1: How strong are we at making Big Requests of each other? How well do we work together so that the requests are clearly linked to what we are up to together? Also, how strong are we at making Big Requests of others outside the team?

Conversation 2: How well do we work with each other between meetings to maximise the probability of success? Do we collaborate well with each other to draw the best from each other? Do we exchange information to make sure everyone is in the loop on progress, roadblocks and how we're going to adjust to get round them?

Conversation 3: How well do we acknowledge successes along the way? How openly do we acknowledge each other? How well do we build on successes by imagining new possibilities? How regularly do we celebrate to help keep the energy strong?

Conversation 3a: How well do we speak straight when the team underperforms? How well do we keep out of 'blame' and in 'what can we learn and how shall we proceed?' How quickly do we re-energise as a team after setbacks?

Conversation 4: How robust are we at setting a new timeline and working to it? And how well do we ensure we apply the learning from any underperformance?

I've often found that members of a team who explore this framework together can take their ability to deliver to whole new levels.

> "Resonant leaders know when to be collaborative and when to be visionary, when to listen and when to command. These leaders naturally nurture relationships, surface simmering issues, and create the human synergies of a group in harmony."
>
> Goleman, Boyatzis and McKee

In summary ...

Future–Engage–Deliver is a plain and simple framework that can help you get the best from your teams. When they are at their best, teams have a strong sense of

"We Are Up To Something Together."

And this involves each of Future, Engage and Deliver:

- **Future** is where the 'Something' is co-invented,
- **Engage** is where 'Together' is cemented, and
- **Deliver** is where the 'Something' is made real through working 'Together'.

When a team isn't working well together, there will be something missing in Future, Engage or Deliver, and probably in one of the first two. Another lens to use is that of The Four Energies. Notice what energy is missing and bring it. And finally be At Your Best and help others be that way too.

Best wishes for the journey with your teams.

AMANDA MACKENZIE

Amanda Mackenzie is Chief Marketing & Communications Officer at Aviva. As well as her day job, she's a non-executive director at Mothercare, on the board of the National Youth Orchestra and the President of the Marketing Society. Phew!

She faced some real challenges when she joined Aviva. The main task was to influence the business in all continents by setting up the company's first global marketing function in a culture that didn't believe it needed one. Plus there was the immediate challenge of moving established brand names like Norwich Union to Aviva. The only way this could be done was through a team approach.

Amanda describes how FED helped the team come together and rapidly build momentum.

'First what was brilliant was that FED gave us a map and a common language that helped us see what the steps in the journey were. This immediately helped everyone in the team feel less daunted and more confident to get started.

'Second, exploring the Engage part of leading helped us quickly build the relationships in the team and navigate the relationship-based issues that arose from us trying to bring people with us. You know, issues are rarely in what needs to be done. They're mostly in the relationships and to what extent people are engaged or not.

'What was particularly great was that FED helped us break into the established network of relationships. So rather than just "going for a beer", conversations were purposeful because they were all about building a common future together.

'And I'm delighted to say that all this helped us deliver what we set out to achieve including a brand that is now more positively viewed and well known than Norwich Union ever was and in the top 10 most valuable brands in the UK. Also we've won numerous awards and a lot of the business gained off the back of a team "being up to something together", one of Steve's great phrases.

Future–Engage–Deliver
and **Organisations**

The way that organisations can truly excel is by encouraging and developing leadership at all levels – help everyone be the CEO of something!

- Future–Engage–Deliver and **Organisations**
- Led by the top team
- Not Led from the Top
- And two final ideas

People regularly say to me, 'Ok, I can now easily see how FED works for individuals and teams but how do we get it to make a difference across our whole organisation?' So here are some thoughts for two types of reader – those of you whose remit currently includes improving the performance of an organisation and those of you whose remit doesn't but you've decided it will do as part of what you're up to!

So don't be held back by titles, hierarchy and what you make organisation charts mean. If you want the organisation that you work in to succeed, then choose to do something about it. This chapter may give you some ideas about how to go about it.

Future–Engage–Deliver and Organisations

First, let me be clear. When I say 'organisation', I'm thinking of anything bigger than one team. It can be a department in a business, school or hospital. It can be a business unit or an organisation in total. The goal is to have large groups of people work brilliantly individually and together to lift the performance of the whole.

Just imagine for a moment what it would be like if everyone in your organisation was clear about and engaged in the Future you're building, and feeling that you're all up to something together. There'd be no silos or one part at odds or disconnected from another. People would have high ambitions not just for their local teams but for the organisation as a whole. People would be conscious of whether relationships were big enough to get the job done and, if they weren't, they'd get on with building them. And people would get to the real conversations quickly because there was a common language for leadership everywhere just like there is a common language for finance or marketing or strategy.

We are proud to have helped some organisations move to this special place. Not surprisingly, we would say that the key ingredient has been leadership but we don't mean just leadership at the top. We mean leadership at all levels.

Again, beware being sucked back into the old story of organisations – that there is leadership only at the top and the rest of us just follow! No, the way that organisations can truly excel is by encouraging and developing leadership at all levels – everyone is the CEO of something!

So what's involved in bringing out the best from everyone to have an organisation perform much closer to what's possible? We have seen two routes taken. One starts with the leadership at the top. The other doesn't rely on this. It comes about from the energy of people anywhere in an organisation lighting fires that then spread. Let's look at each route in turn.

> "In winning organisations, people seem to have more energy. And they consciously work at creating positive energy in everyone else in the organisation."
>
> Noel Tichy

Led by the top team

The fastest way forward starts by having a top team be brilliant at practising FED. That is, there is an aligned top team up to something together. This sounds straightforward enough but we don't always find it in place and at times we've even found resistance to becoming united from some members of the team. Part of the issue can be that senior teams are often populated by life-long go-getters whose ambition has been to be the Leader of a Part and they don't want to give this up.

But it's vital not to cut corners at this stage. In all organisations, there seems to be lots of 'board-watching', that is, careful watching of the senior leaders' every move. People are constantly watching for signs of are they a team? Are they giving out the same message? Do they support each other? Do they get on? Are the relationships big enough? And so on. If you want an aligned organisation, you absolutely must have an aligned top team.

The chapter on FED and Teams can be an excellent guide to the ground a top team must cover to ensure they're aligned on everything that's important. And I'd pull out two topics for special attention. The first is that a top team in an organisation should grasp the opportunity to not only envisage the future they want but also the culture that'll be needed to get there.

Being clear on just the vision, the strategy and the structure is never enough. We've found a clear statement of the culture or desired behaviours or ways of working is essential if fastest progress is to be made.

But second, and of course more importantly, each of this top team will then need to be seen as a walking example of this culture, including being an engaging ambassador who will energise and bring in others to build the future. This may require some one-on-one work to support each leader in reaching this level. Again, I say don't cut corners at this stage.

The engagement of people outside the top team can then take two paths. Some organisations benefit most by engagement then happening along department lines. That is, each member of the top team has sessions with their reports to build the alignment and develop each other as leaders. Some organisations need much stronger relationships across the functions, so this next level of engagement happens in cross-functional groups. Either way, our preferred way of introducing FED is over a period of time, rather than as a one-off intervention. This is to give plenty of opportunity for the most important part of any FED leadership programme – the practice back at work.

After this stage, we then recommend that a top leadership group is formed – usually 40–70 in a large organisation and less in a smaller one. This group we sometimes call a Community of Leaders can be a very powerful force for change. It's made clear to all in this community that the organisation needs them to be leaders and crucially Leaders of the Whole, not just of their parts. We've worked with some leaders who have wanted to pull together this group earlier but we've seen it fall flat. The reason is that the bigger the group, the much more difficult it is to truly 'engage' participants. Yes, it's possible to 'communicate to and tell' but engagement happens much faster in smaller groups. So we say pull this bigger group together but only after each member has been previously engaged in a smaller group session.

Creating and galvanising this wider leadership group can significantly accelerate the pace and depth of change. There are now dozens of leaders leading for the whole rather than just the handful in a typical top team. Projects and initiatives requiring cross-functional working move at a much faster pace. And there are now many more ambassadors for the future to get out and engage others.

This rolling model of engaged leaders engaging others to join in and step forward as leaders can then be spread further through the organisation. People sometimes ask, 'How do we cascade FED?' My reply is always, 'What we'll help you cascade is your leadership'.

That is, it is always the leadership in the room that matters not the models or handouts. With careful planning, fully engaged leaders can spark a sort of leadership that eventually comes alive throughout the organisation.

But then crucially this new leadership needs active support to avoid it quietly fading as the pressures of today swamp it. This is best done in three ways. First, we develop in-house champions for leadership so that individuals and teams have someone on hand to give them an injection of FED when they need one.

Second, we encourage that the desired leadership behaviours become part of the systems of the organisation, for example the appraisal process, 360 degree and employee surveys. That way, leading becomes some of the fabric of how we do things around here.

And third, and most importantly, we support the senior leaders to keep 'how are we leading round here?' a regular, active topic of conversation for all in the organisation. It's too easy to spend all our time exploring the 'what' of what we're doing and forget to keep the 'how' of how we're doing it front of mind. Shifting this balance can have a huge impact on how people, and ultimately an organisation, performs.

"Lasting improvement does not take place by pronouncements or official programmes. Culture is changed by focusing on our own actions in the small, barely-noticed activities of our work. In a way, the only culture that exists for us is in the room in which we are standing at the moment. It is the transformation of the culture of the room we are in that holds the possibility of transforming the culture of the rest of the organisation. It is change from the inside out."

Peter Block

Not Led from the Top

But what if there isn't initially any visible leadership from the top for widespread development of leadership? Well, you simply start somewhere else!

I'm delighted to report that we have seen some brilliant examples of people not at the most senior levels of an organisation sparking interest and then action with their colleagues and clients. One of our guidelines when working in big organisations is 'go with the energy'. That is, there will always be some people more urgent and ready to dive into the leadership space than others. We have learned to support them in lighting a fire and helping it spread.

For example, in the Future chapter (Chapter 3) of this book, I told the story of Stephen, an HR manager at the time. He wanted his organisation to succeed so he regularly met with or wrote to his Chief Executive, Richard, nudging him about the leadership or lack of it that he was seeing. This in time led to us running a FED programme for the top several hundred leaders. And as I wrote in that chapter, this led to Richard saying it had made 'a material difference to the ambition, culture and performance of the company'. All because the scope of what one person was up to included the success of his organisation. Check in on yourself for a moment:

- What would it look like if you started more fires?
- Who else could well be ready to join you?
- How much does the leadership of your organisation matter to you?
- How could you be influencing it more than you do currently?

> "By the time we reach puberty, the world has shaped us to a greater extent than we realise. Our family, friends, and society in general have told us – by word and example – how to be. But people begin to become leaders at that moment when they decide for themselves how to be."
>
> Warren Bennis

And two final ideas

I have tried to give you an idea of what's involved practically in having FED help transform the performance of an organisation. And at the same time, there are two higher-level ideas we always keep in mind when helping steer an organisation to greatness.

The first idea is one of those that stopped me in my tracks when I first saw it. I read it in an article by Ghoshal and Bruck summarising their research into what makes an effective leader. They found that the focus of truly effective leader/managers was:

> 'to fulfill personal goals that tally with those of the organisation as a whole'.

That is, they were not fulfilling organisation goals that made them feel good. They were first and foremost 'fulfilling personal goals'. Now this can feel threatening to the old-fashioned leader but we've been here already. In the Engage chapter (Chapter 4) I pointed to a shift that leaders of organisations need to make but sometimes don't. I wrote:

> 'In Engage, the key is to spark Possibilities in others that are meaningful to them. This is a shift of focus many leaders don't figure out. They can be excited about the Future and can automatically assume others will be too. Sometimes others might be. But what you've really got to do is help people see Possibilities for themselves and what they care about in what's being explored.'

This is one of the great 'Both/Ands' to pull off. Leading an organisation, you have to **both** be up to something yourself **and** encourage others to be up to something too.

This combination is captured brilliantly by the second idea. Someone once said he wanted the people in his organisation to be 'unbridled yet corralled'. That is, there is a corral, vision, strategy or goal that we will work inside of. However, inside of that, be up to something and go for it. This is such a good lens through which to look at leaders and where they are strong and not. For a minute, think about yourself:

- Are you great at setting out a clear corral?

- Do you make the corral even stronger by inviting others in to co-invent it and build it with you?

- How great are you at helping others be unbridled?

- What would it look like if your intent was to come in every day and help people be unbridled?

Few of us will be able to say we are brilliant in all of these areas. But as ever we can get better with practice. And what about the most senior leaders in your organisation? Do they need help with these questions? How could exploring these ideas improve the quality of their leadership?

In summary

We must not be held back by the old thinking about leadership and organisations which tells us that leadership exists only at the top. It is the time for clearer thinking about how we get organisations to work and I believe leadership at all levels is a huge part of the answer. Robert Greenleaf, famous for his idea of Servant Leadership, makes the point strongly:

> 'Who is holding back more rapid movement to the better society that is reasonable and possible with available resources? Who is responsible for the mediocre performance of so many of our institutions? Not evil people. Not stupid people. Not apathetic people. Not the "system". The real enemy is fuzzy thinking on the part of good, intelligent, vital people, and their failure to lead.'

I meet 'good, intelligent, vital people' every week. My encouragement always is to please use the simple ideas in FED to clarify your 'fuzzy thinking' and make sure you aren't 'failing to lead'!

BRAND LEARNING

Mhairi McEwan and Andy Bird are the founding partners of Brand Learning, the leading global consultancy in building marketing capabilities. While they have been passionate about growing the business at home and abroad, it's also been important to them that it's been done in a certain way, focused on valuing and developing their people while creating a great place to work. So it was no surprise in 2011 when they won the award for The Sunday Times Best Small Company to Work For.

I first met Andy years ago when we were co-leading the Marketing Society's Marketing Leadership Programme. He saw the difference FED was making to the participants and wanted Brand Learning to benefit too. It's been a privilege working with Mhairi and Andy, two leaders who embody so much of what FED is about. As they put it,

'The key value of FED to our team has been the way it has provided a common language we can all use to build our personal relationships. By opening up deeper, more honest conversations about how people feel working together, we have been able to grow both as individuals and as a team.

'We have used FED not just with our leadership team, but throughout the organisation. By having everyone sharing in the understanding of the key ideas and concepts, people across the company have been able to play a role in supporting the personal development and success of those around them. It's made a big difference to the openness of our culture.'

Conclusion

I hope by now you'll be a lot clearer on what you are up to and how you go about making it happen. You'll also by now have a good idea of what I'm up to.

I believe leadership is the one ingredient above all others that has organisations prosper and people be at their best more of the time. But there are too many people struggling to get their arms round this topic of leadership and even more who don't even see themselves as leaders.

I want to change all that. My ambition is to have people who, regardless of position or title, know how to grow themselves and others as leaders. And I want a Future in which 'how are we leading this place and how can we do it better?' is an explicit and regular conversation throughout organisations.

So please use this book as a prompt both in developing yourself and others and whenever you can start new conversations in your organisation about the quality of its leadership. Help start a movement towards better quality leadership everywhere.

I believe the key is 'keep it simple'! We've been making leadership seem a lot more complicated and exclusive than it needs to be. Rather than lots of theory, I believe all you need are a few big ideas and lots of practice.

Here then is the final summary of the big ideas in *Future–Engage–Deliver*, the only three leadership practices you'll ever need.

Future

1   You are up to something! There is a Future you want that is connected to what you care about and that Future guides who you are and what you do today.

2 You step back and see the bigger picture. You are constantly aware of and managing the context, the overall situation.

3 And this practice helps you keep out of Operator/Manager Mode. Yes, you'll have to spend some time there but you won't be there more than you need be.

4 You'll help yourself spend even more time in Leader Mode by having a clear picture of who you want to be as a leader.

5 And all this keeps your Spirit Energy alive and sparks it in others.

Engage

1 Every day you look for opportunities to engage others in the Future you are building. And your conscious intent is to 'engage' not just 'transmit at' or 'tell'.

2 You use the Levels of Engagement. You think about who is at what level and the level you want them at.

3 You recognise that your engaging happens inside your relationships. So you're always building your relationships so they are big enough to get the job done.

4 You help yourself by asking for feedback so you learn more about the Light you bring and the Shadow you cast.

5 And in all this you are learning to bring and harness the power of Emotional Energy that often remains untapped.

Deliver

1 First you make sure you're looking to deliver through others.

2 You bring your resolve and commitment to what you want to deliver now because it is directly linked to the Future you want.

3 You Deliver More Later by actively developing others as leaders, not just good quality followers. You do this because you are committed to others' success and the long-term success of your organisation.

4 And you do all of this through practising The Leader's Conversations for Delivery, creating more Robust Dialogue and particularly making bigger requests.

You turbo-charge your progress in these areas by making your practice Conscious Practice. You learn and grow so much faster by having a full and active Support Team. And you are always looking to go beyond your limits and be At Your Best More of the Time.

You already have the Leadership Muscles to make a bigger difference to your Future. Through regular prompts at **www.futureengagedeliver.com** we will help you keep your practice front of mind. Please also let us know at that address of your progress.

Best wishes and I look forward to hearing from you,
Steve.

And Another 'Thank You'

I am indebted to all those I have read and learned from. And special thanks to those I've quoted from. My thinking has been shaped in particular by the following writers, books and articles. You can see which practice in Future–Engage–Deliver many are linked to by going to the online support pages for the book at **www.futureengagedeliver.com/book**.

Abbey, A. (2008) *Stop Making Excuses and Start Living with Energy*, Chichester: Capstone Publishing Ltd.

Argyris, C. (1994) 'Good Communication that Blocks Learning', *Harvard Business Review*, 72(4): 77–85.

Bennis, W. (1997) *Why Leaders Can't Lead: The Unconscious Conspiracy Continues*, California: Jossey-Bass.

Bennis, W. and Goldsmith, J. (2010) *Learning to Lead: A Workbook on Becoming a Leader*, Cambridge, MA: Basic Books.

Bennis, W. and Ward Biederman, P. (1997) *Organizing Genius: The Secrets of Creative Collaboration*, Cambridge, MA: Perseus Books.

Bennis, W. and Nanus, B. (2003) *Leaders: Strategies for Taking Charge*, New York: Harper Business Essentials.

Bossidy, L., Charan, R. and Burck, C. (2011) *Execution: The Discipline of Getting Things Done*, New York: Random House.

Buckingham, M. and Coffman, C. (2005) *First, Break All the Rules: What the World's Greatest Managers Do Differently*, London: Simon and Schuster.

Collins, J. (2001) *Good to Great: Why Some Companies Make The Leap … And Others Don't*, New York: HarperCollins.

Collins, J. and Porras, J. (1994) *Built to Last: Successful Habits of Visionary Companies*, New York: HarperCollins.

Conger, J. (1998) 'The Necessary Art of Persuasion', *Harvard Business Review*, May/June.

Covey, S. (2004) *The 7 Habits of Highly Effective People: Powerful Lessons in Personal Change*, London: Simon and Schuster.

DePree, M. (2004) *Leadership is an Art*, New York: Crown Business.

Ditzler, J. (2006) *Your Best Year Yet: How To Make the Next 12 Months Your Most Successful Ever!*, London: Harper Element.

Drucker, P. (1999) *Managing for Results*, Oxford: Butterworth-Heinemann.

Dwoskin, H. (2007) *The Sedona Method: Your Key To Lasting Happiness, Success, Peace and Emotional Well-being*, Sedona: Sedona Press.

Ghoshal, S. and Bruch, H. (2002) 'Beware the Busy Manager', *Harvard Business Review*, 80(2): 62–69.

Ghoshal, S. and Bruch, H. (2004) 'Reclaim your Job', *Harvard Business Review*, 82(1): 41–80.

Godin, S. (2008) *Tribes: We Need You To Lead Us*, New York: Portfolio.

Goffee, R. and Jones, G. (2006) *Why Should Anyone Be Led By You?: What It Takes to Be An Authentic Leader*, Boston MA: Harvard Business School Press.

Goldsmith, M. and Morgan, H. (2004) 'Leadership is a Contact Sport: The "Follow-Up" Factor in Management Development', *Strategy + Business*, 36(Fall).

Goleman, D., Boyatzis, D. and McKee, A. (2002) *Primal Leadership: Realizing the Power of Emotional Intelligence*, Boston MA: Harvard Business School Press.

Greenleaf, R.K. (2003) *The Servant-Leader Within: A Transformative Path*, Toronto: Paulist Press International.

Hamel, G. and Prahalad, C.K. (1989) 'Strategic Intent', *Harvard Business Review*, May.

Hamel, G. and Prahalad, C.K. (1993) 'Strategy as Stretch and Leverage', *Harvard Business Review*, March.

Handy, C. (2002) *The Age of Unreason*, Random House Business.

Handy, C. (1998) *The Hungry Spirit: Beyond Capitalism – A Quest for Purpose In The Modern World*, New York: Broadway Books.

Hargrove, R. and Senge, P. (1998) *Mastering the Art of Creative Collaboration*, BusinessWeek Books.

Heider, J. (2005) *The Tao of Leadership: Lao Tze's Tao Te Ching Adapted for a New Age,* Florida: Humanics Publishing Group.

Heifitz, R.A. and Linsky, M. (2002) 'A Survival Guide for Leaders', *Harvard Business Review*, June.

Katzenbach, J.R. and Smith, D.K. (2003) *The Wisdom of Teams: Creating the High Performance Organization*, New York: HarperBusiness Essentials.

Kelley, R.E. (1988) 'Management by Whose Objectives', *Harvard Business Review*, Nov/Dec.

Kotter, J. (1999) 'What Effective General Managers Really Do', *Harvard Business Review*, March/April.

Kotter, J. (2007) 'Leading Change: Why Transformation Efforts Fail', *Harvard Business Review*, Jan.

Kouzes, J. and Posner, B. (2007) *The Leadership Challenge, 4th edition*, California: Jossey-Bass.

Loehr, J. and Schwartz, T. (2003) *On Form: Achieving High Energy Performance Without Sacrificing Health and Happiness and Life Balance*, London: Nicholas Brealey Publishing.

Macleod, D. and Brady, C. (2007) *The Extra Mile: How To Engage Your People to Win*, Harlow: Financial Times Prentice Hall.

Mintzberg, H. (2004) *Managers not MBAs: A Hard Look at the Soft Practice of Managing and Management Development*, Harlow: Financial Times Prentice Hall.

Owen, Harrison (1999) *The Spirit of Leadership: Liberating the Leader in Each of Us*, California: Berrett-Koehler Publishers, Inc.

Owen, Harrison (2000) *The Power of Spirit: How Organizations Transform*, California: Berrett-Koehler Publishers, Inc.

Owen, Hilarie (2000) *In Search of Leaders*, Chichester: John Wiley and Sons, Ltd.

Parks, S.D. (2005) *Leadership Can Be Taught: A Bold Approach for a Complex World*, Boston MA: Harvard Business School Press.

Pascale, R.T. (1990) *Managing on the Edge: Companies that Use Conflict to Stay Ahead*, New York: Simon and Schuster.

Pearce, T. (2003) *Leading out Loud: Inspiring Change Through Authentic Communication*, California: Jossey-Bass.

Robinson, G. (2004) *I'll Show Them Who's Boss: The Six Secrets of Highly Effective Management*, London: BBC Books.

Rogers, C. R. (1996) *A Way of Being*, Boston, MA: Houghton Mifflin.

Rogers, C.R. and Freiberg, J.H. (1994) *Freedom to Learn, 3rd edition*, Harlow: Pearson Prentice Hall.

Rosenberg, M.B. (2003) *Nonviolent Communication: A Language of Life, 2nd edition*, Encinitas, CA: PuddleDancer Press.

Schaffer, R. (2000) 'Demand Better Results – and Get Them', *Harvard Business Review*, August.

Schein, E.H. (2010) *Organizational Culture and Leadership, 4th edition*, California: Jossey-Bass.

Senge, P. (2006) *The Fifth Discipline: Art and Practice of the Learning Organization, 2nd edition,* London: Random House Business.

Smith, C.E. (1997) *The Merlin Factor: Keys to the Corporate Kingdom*, Surrey: Ashgate Publishing.

Syed, M. (2010) *Bounce: How Champions are Made*, London: Fourth Estate.

Thaler, R.H. and Sunstein, C.R. (2009) *Nudge: Improving Decisions about Health, Wealth and Happiness*, London: Penguin Books.

Tichy, N.M. (2002) *The Leadership Engine: How Winning Companies Build Leaders At Every Level*, New York: Basingstoke: Harper Business Essentials.

Townend, A. (2007) *Assertiveness and Diversity*, Palgrave.

Vicere, A.A. and Fulmer, R.M. (1997) *Leadership by Design: How Benchmark Companies Sustain Success Through Investment in Continuous Learning*, Harvard Business School Press.

Wheatley, M.J. (2006) *Leadership and the New Science: Discovering Order in a Chaotic World, 3rd edition,* California: Berrett-Koehler Publishers, Inc.

Whyte, D. (2002) *The Heart Aroused: Poetry and the Preservation of the Soul in Corporate America*, New York: Doubleday.

Zaleznik, A. (1997) 'Managers and Leaders: Are they different?', *Harvard Business Review*, May.

Zander, R.S. and Zander, B. (2006) *The Art of Possibility: Transforming Professional and Personal Life*, London: Penguin Books.

Index

Read on

9780273732044

9780273729860

9780273751328

9780273759614